YOUR MIND MATTERS

Also available in the Pioneer *Perspectives* series:

Better Than or Equal To?	Linda Harding
Caring for New Christians	Margaret Ellis
Prophecy in the Church	Martin Scott
Radical Evangelism	Pete Gilbert
Relationships—Jesus Style	Stuart Lindsell
The Role and Ministry of Women	Martin Scott
The Worshipping Church	Noel Richards

For further information on the Pioneer *Perspectives* series and Pioneer, please write to:

P.O. Box 79c, Esher, Surrey, KT10 9LP

YOUR MIND MATTERS

Developing a Biblical View of the World

Chris Seaton

WORD PUBLISHING
Nelson Word Ltd
Milton Keynes, England

WORD AUSTRALIA
Kilsyth, Victoria, Australia

WORD COMMUNICATIONS LTD
Vancouver, B.C., Canada

STRUIK CHRISTIAN BOOKS (PTY) LTD
Maitland, South Africa

CHRISTIAN MARKETING NEW ZEALAND LTD
Havelock North, New Zealand

JENSCO LTD
Hong Kong

JOINT DISTRIBUTORS SINGAPORE–
ALBY COMMERCIAL ENTERPRISES PTE LTD
and
CAMPUS CRUSADE
SALVATION BOOK CENTRE
Malaysia

YOUR MIND MATTERS

© Pioneer 1993.

Published by Nelson Word Ltd./Pioneer 1993.

All rights reserved. No part of this publication may be reproduced or transmitted in any form or by any means, electronic or mechanical, including photocopying, recording, or any information storage or retrieval system, without permission in writing from the publisher.

ISBN 0-85009-732-0   (Australia ISBN 1-86258-277-7)

Unless otherwise indicated, Scripture quotations are from the HOLY BIBLE, NEW INTERNATIONAL VERSION (NIV). Copyright © 1973, 1978, 1984 by International Bible Society.
Other quotations are from the King James Version of the Bible.

The quotation on pp. 68–69 is from Snyder, Howard, *Liberating the Church* (Marshall Pickering, 1983), permission applied for.

Front cover illustration: *Mas à Saintes-Mairies*, Vincent Van Gogh, courtesy of Christie's, London/Bridgeman Art Library (detail).

Printed in Finland for Nelson Word Ltd. by WSOY.

93 94 95 96 / 10 9 8 7 6 5 4 3 2 1

FOREWORD

Pioneer *Perspectives* are perhaps more than their title suggests!

They are carefully researched presentations of material, on important issues, appealing to thinking churches, creative leaders and responsible Christians.

Each *Perspective* pioneers in as much as it is at the cutting edge of biblical and theological issues. Each will continue to pioneer with new ideas, concepts and data drawn from Scripture, history and a contemporary understanding of both.

They are perspectives in as much as they aim to be an important contribution to the ongoing debate on issues such as women in ministry and leadership; prophets and prophecy in the church; biblical models of evangelism; integrating and discipling new believers; growing and building local churches and further perspectives on Christ's second coming.

Importantly, these studies use a journal style of presentation, and are written by people who are currently working out the implications of the issues they are writing about, in local churches. This is vital if we are to escape the dangerous fantasy of abstract theology without practical experience. They are not written to contribute to the paralysis of analysis—rather to feed, strengthen, nurture and inform so that we can be equipped to get God's will done, by networking the nations with the gospel using all the resources that are available to us.

God's Word is always an event. How much we

thank Him that He has left us an orderly account of what He wants us to believe, how He wants us to live, and what He wants us to do in order to bring heaven to the earth. As we embrace a better understanding of Scripture, rooted in local church, national and international mission, we shall become a part of the great eschatological purpose of bringing back the King—not for a church defeated, cowering and retiring but for one which, despite colossal odds, pressures and persecutions, is faithful to her Lord and His Word. To do that we must 'search the Scriptures' to see if many of these 'new things' are true. I commend these *Perspectives* to you as they are published on a regular basis throughout these coming years.

Gerald Coates
Director Pioneer Trust/Team Leader

Pioneer consists of a team and network of churches, committed to dynamic and effective biblical Christianity.

The national team act as advisers and consultants to churches, which in many cases develop into a partnership with the Pioneer team. These are the churches keen to identify with the theology, philosophy, ethos and purpose of Pioneer. The team have a vigorous youth ministry, church-planting strategy and evangelistic emphasis.

Training courses include Equipped to Lead, Emerging Leaders and the highly successful TIE teams (Training In Evangelism).

Pioneer have also been instrumental in initiating and funding March for Jesus (with Ichthus/YWAM); Jubilee Campaign (for the suffering church worldwide); and ACET (Aids Care Education Training).

ACKNOWLEDGEMENTS

Many thanks to all my friends in Revelation who have been a part of my spiritual up-bringing—Roger and Maggie Ellis, Dave and Lucy Evans, Murray Jacobs, Mark and Rachel Searle, Mike and Alison Wilkerson and many others. Thanks also to colleagues in Pioneer who have encouraged me in this project, especially Steve and Ann Clifford and Martin Scott. Thanks to Gerard Kelly and Jonny Baker: two friends with whom 'iron sharpened iron' on this subject and who first got me thinking about what 'having a world view' means. Jonny once again gave some insightful and encouraging comments on the manuscript.

Very special thanks to my lovely wife, Charlotte, who has been a constant friend and a constant challenge to my lifestyle. Above all, thanks to two of my heroes who have shaped my thinking more than any others—Gerald Coates and Mike Morris.

Chris Seaton
May 1993

CONTENTS

INTRODUCTION		13
Exercise 1:	A Questionnaire	17
CHAPTER 1:	**The Way We See the World**	21
CHAPTER 2:	**A Biblical World View**	29
Exercise 2:	A Biblical Case Study	47
CHAPTER 3:	**Tackling Dualism**	51
CHAPTER 4:	**Thinking Straight for Jesus' Sake**	75
APPENDIX 1:	Glossary of Terms	93
APPENDIX 2:	Bibliography	96

INTRODUCTION

It was after the successful Pioneer Solent conference, 'Towards an Effective Church 1988', that a number of church leaders met in a pub in the South Downs to review the event and suggest ideas for its sequel. Amidst the fine food and delicious ale, one of my few constructive contributions to the gathering was to suggest that we should look at the environment during the forthcoming conference. It was, after all, that *annus mirabilis* of the Green movement in Britain, 1989.

A few weeks later I was quite surprised to receive an invitation from Kevin Allan to address a seminar on the subject of 'How Green is Your Gospel?' This was the first time that I had begun to think seriously about green issues from a biblical point of view. After the generous reception given to that talk, Mike Morris then suggested that I write a book on the same subject towards the end of 1990. Between then and the publication of the book *Whose Earth?* in summer 1992, I spent a great deal of time reading and thinking about the Bible, the Church and ecology.

However, the more closely I looked at the way in which the Church was responding to green issues, the more I realised that, in Phil Vogel's words, 'the issue is not the issue'. As far as the environment is concerned, the real issue facing Christians is not so much stewardship of creation, but *how we think*. I began to see that the way in which we respond to different challenges and make crucial decisions is determined by the way in which we view and understand the world around us.

I also began to see that most of us have been partly shaped by influences that are not entirely godly and yet which can be very hard to discern. In particular, I became aware of a phenomenon known as 'dualism': the idea that there is a sacred realm and a secular one; a public realm and a private one; a physical realm and a spiritual one. Dualism has, I believe, infected large parts of the Church with a kind of spiritual schizophrenia and is one of its main enemies today. Unless we expose it, unlearn it and live more wholistically,[1] then our gospel will not be the culturally relevant message it needs to be, and our view of the world may not truly reflect our beliefs.

In the light of all this, I grew concerned that unless some hard questions were asked about how we use our minds, we might actually miss some of our most precious goals and fail to see our fondest dreams fulfilled. With the support and encouragement of many friends and colleagues on the Pioneer Team, this Pioneer *Perspective* has been written in an attempt to address some of these concerns. You may not agree with everything you read in this book, but I pray that it will be a provocation to think through the issues raised. For integrity's sake I want to make it clear that I have communicated quite a lot of ideas and beliefs which are beyond where I'm living at present, but I have written with sincerity and a desire to live in everything God shows me.

In a few thousand words it is hard to know where to begin on the huge subject of the state of the Christian mind. The means I have chosen is to consider the subject of our world view. As we look carefully at the way in which most of us learn to view the world and examine

---

[1]. I prefer to spell the word with a 'w' to emphasise wholeness and distinguish it from 'holism' which has pantheistic and New Age overtones.

the heart of a truly biblical world view, I hope we can make a start.

Your mind *does* matter terribly to God, and is hugely important to the way you live out your Christian faith. The French thinker Blaise Pascal said, 'Working hard to think clearly is the beginning of moral conduct.' I will use his words as an excuse if you find this Pioneer *Perspective* hard going! Writing on the Christian thinking does sound like a cure for insomnia, but I passionately believe it should be an exciting subject. I hope that some of this excitement comes over as I have tried to make the book as readable as possible, but only you can judge whether or not I have succeeded. If you have the time and the inclination I think you will get the best from this book if you read it through twice.

Exercise 1

A QUESTIONNAIRE

This questionnaire is designed to be answered as honestly and as fully as possible before you read any further. It is not an attempt to trick you but will hopefully demonstrate something about your world view as a Christian before we start.

1. As a Christian, what is your reason for living?

   _____

   _____

   _____

2. How would you describe the essence of the Christian gospel?

   _____

   _____

   _____

3. What do you think the Church should be aiming to do?

   _____

   _____

   _____

18 Your Mind Matters

4. List ten different ways in which you have changed since becoming a Christian.

   _____
   _____
   _____

5. When you think about heaven, what do you look forward to most?

   _____
   _____
   _____

6. What would you be doing now if sin had not entered the world?

   _____
   _____
   _____

7. What is the most important thing to you in life? (not what you think *should* be most important to you!)

   _____
   _____
   _____

8. How do you feel about your job/studies/current situation?

   _____
   _____
   _____

9. What is the most fulfilling thing in your life?

_____

_____

_____

10. What are you dreaming to do for God?

_____

_____

_____

I will not be giving any answers to these questions: clearly many of them are highly subjective anyway. You will find out some of my thoughts on these subjects in the last chapter.

CHAPTER 1

THE WAY WE SEE THE WORLD

What on earth is this world view?

In the Introduction I used one of those buzz-words which has become quite fashionable of late, but which few of us can usually define. That phrase is 'world view'. Throughout this book I will be using it with regularity because it best describes the central theme I am considering. It has a kind of trendy, sociological ring to it and can sound rather vague. For the sake of clarity I want to begin by explaining what I mean by world view.

Put in metaphors, a world view is a map and compass which helps us to know where we are. It enables us to interpret reality and understand life. It is the framework of ideas around which we build our vision of the world in which we live. It is the lens through which we see and make sense of everything.

Everybody has a world view and it is this which enables us to steer through the murky and complex waters of life, relationships and, as Christians, the Bible itself. Each world view has been shaped by a number of different influences. These influences will include a combination of factors such as the culture of which we are a part, our education, parenting, life experiences, friendships, personal preferences and so on. World views cannot be denied, but they can be changed.

A world view can be seen as the bedrock of what

forms a society—the ideas and values that make a group of people tick and gel together. Look at any society—whether a nation state, a local church or a pack of cub scouts—and you will find a mutual world view there, to some degree.

Of course, there will be individuals who are the exception within every society, but the world view of a community will be that which the majority culture shares. A clashing of world views will happen wherever there is a strong resistance to the dominant world view by any minority. The rebellious and outrageous expressions of fashion, music, lifestyle and occasionally violence which occurred in Britain, France and North America during the late 1960s are an example of this sort of clash. Something similar—if somewhat less idealistic—happened again in Britain during the late 1970s in what became known as the 'punk era'. In these cases it was the younger generations who were challenging the world view of their parents over such issues as conformity, thrift and the ethics of work, capitalism and sexual behaviour.

Similar world view clashes are induced by the presence of immigrant communities within a nation. The Salman Rushdie affair is a fascinating example of the way in which different cultures place value on different things. For the Muslim, the Qur'an is a Holy Book and, to that world view, nothing is of greater importance apart from Allah himself. To blaspheme against the Qur'an is properly punishable by death—such a punishment is very reasonable. This response inspires outrage in the minds of most white, secular, liberal Britons whose humanistic world view places nothing higher than the life of an individual.

Who is right in these clashes? However open, reasonable and broad-minded we like to think we are, our judgements and opinions will be shaped by our value system and by our own world view. It is quite impossible to say who is right and who is not on these matters without assuming the existence of one particular world view or another.

Faith

You can see how a world view works by the way in which it walks. Brian Walsh and Richard Middleton, in the book which has proved seminal in helping Christians to think about this issue,[1] suggest that a world view can never just be a vision *of* life, but it must also be a vision *for* life. In other words, it is not just about *understanding* how any group lives, but it will also *motivate* that group in how they live.

Walsh and Middleton go on to say that when pared down, a world view is basically a faith commitment. That is, it is about the way in which any individual will answer four basic questions:

WHO AM I?—or what is the nature of my humanity and what is the nature of my task and purpose as a human?

WHERE AM I?—what is the nature of the universe and of the world in which I live?

WHAT'S THE PROBLEM?— what is the nature of evil, and how do I overcome the obstacles to my fulfilment?

---
1. *The Transforming Vision* (IVP, 1984).

WHAT'S THE REMEDY?—how do I overcome these hindrances, or what is the nature of salvation?

Perhaps it would be helpful to take a snapshot of just two world views which we see around us and look at them in the light of their faith commitments. These definitions are my own and are not authoritative, simply giving context to the idea of conflicting world views:

A *Sun* reader

As the *Sun* is the most widely read newspaper in the land, perhaps this reflects the dominant world view of contemporary Britain.

Firstly, it is profoundly secular because it is non-spiritual (and specifically post-Christian), although it touches its forelock to the status quo of ceremonial religion as part of the state structure. Secondly, it is humanist because in rejecting God and the supernatural the interests of humanity come before anything else. Thirdly, it is rational because in rejecting the supernatural the human mind becomes the reference point by and against which all reality is understood. It could well be argued that the combination of these three encourage the more 'basic instincts' of humanity—sexism and sexual exploitation, racism and prejudice, nationalism and xenophobia, excess and lust—which have become part of the *Sun*'s stock in trade.

This, I believe, could be seen as the faith commitment of one of its followers:

> 'I am me, an individual, the free and independent master of my own destiny. The world I live in is a jungle—full of good things that I am trying to get my hands on so that I can enjoy life. The problem with this jungle is that it is also full of people who are trying to stop me enjoying life. I am also frustrated by my ignorance of nature and lack of tools

for controlling it. My hope rests in the good life of progress where nature gives its bounty for human benefit, and in my own struggle to defeat my enemies. Only then will I find happiness in a life of material wealth, with no needs and no dependence.'

New Age

In marked contrast, the New Age world view could be described as post-materialist. It is essentially a rejection of the spiritually-impoverished world view of humanism and the supposedly archaic and narrow-minded perspectives of the monotheistic religions (that is, Christianity, Judaism and Islam). We have become well-taught on the New Age movement in recent years and recognise that its 'new' spiritual framework is little more than an amalgam and re-working of pagan, Eastern and occult spirituality. I would suggest that its faith commitment runs something like this:

> 'I am me, bearer of infinite personal potential as an integral part of all reality. I am a part of Gaia, the living organism which is planetary home to all life on this earth. Gaia is my mother and she gives me life. Lack of enlightenment, destructive philosophies and paternalistic religions have caused us to lose touch with our true self-awareness and to abuse Gaia. Salvation comes as I truly realise myself and become harmonised with the unity of all things. Meanwhile there will be a period of suffering while Gaia wreaks her revenge and makes her own adjustments following humanity's careless damage.'

Naturally, there are many other examples which could be drawn out and it is a useful exercise to consider what constitutes the basic faith commitment of different cultures, groups and individuals. On the smallest scale it is quite fascinating to do this by listening to the lyrics of a pop song, looking at a painting or reading a book—all these works reveal a world view at work.

All Change!

Most interesting and esoteric stuff this, but what is its relevance for us as Christians? Quite simply, it is relevant because biblical Christians have a message of change to proclaim to the world. The demand of the gospel is first of all to repent . . . 'Jesus began to preach, "Repent, for the kingdom of heaven is near" ' (Matt. 4:17). The Greek word μετανοεω, translated in the New Testament as 'repent' is made up of two source words. The first is μετα, which means 'after' and implies change and the other, ανοεω, means 'to perceive' and is from the root word for 'mind'. Put together, μετανοεω means 'to change one's mind after thought'.[2]

This is not a radical exegesis of what is a familiar Bible word. What I want to suggest, however, is that the concept of repentance is not just about turning from the more obvious of moral errors. It is not simply about cleaning up our lives, choosing to walk God's way rather than our own and thinking pure thoughts rather than impure—important and right though all these are. Instead, repentance is surely about the Word of God and the demands of His Kingdom bringing a fundamental challenge to our world view.

Whether that world view could best be described as occult, Buddhist, New Age, communist, scientific materialistic or just plain old *Sun* reader, 'the axe' must

---

[2]. *Vine's Dictionary of New Testament Words* (Macdonald, n.d.) pp. 961, 962.

be laid to 'the root of the trees' (Matt. 3:10). This kind of root repentance is indeed radical because once we change the framework of our perceptions, once we alter the lens through which we understand life, then profound change will inevitably follow.

Thus, true conversion to Christ should invariably lead to the most almighty clashing of world views. As the new Christian's account of his first conversation with God goes, ' . . . then God said to me, "We're incompatible and I don't change" '! Which of us was compatible with God when we first turned to the Lord? As soon as we decide to follow Christ there is going to be a warring of world views, of which the conflicts between the old sinful nature and the new godly nature are but a part. Our moral choices, like those of the Israelites before us (see Deuteronomy 28), will determine which world view wins, and under which regime we live.

Conclusion

This leads us to ask two important questions of our evangelism and discipling. Firstly, as we preach a message of repentance, are we clearly helping people to step away from the entire framework of their previous world view? Or are we instead simply approaching repentance on a superficial or piecemeal basis? Even if we are very thorough in helping new Christians to turn from living for themselves to living for God, then much of a new believer's world view may not get challenged for many years, if ever. If we simply address the issues of people's behaviour, morality and attitudes—which are essential—but fail to examine the way in which they think, there may be a flaw in discipleship. As a world view is a faith commitment, some of these basic commitments must be renounced, whilst others will not necessarily be inconsistent with following Jesus.

Secondly, once there has been a clear and complete repentance from sin, and from one's pre-Christian world view to boot, what are we encouraging new Christians to commit their faith to? Naturally, one might say, to Jesus Christ, to the Scriptures and to the Kingdom of God. True, but what does that mean in terms of the four questions which make up the faith commitment? As I suggested in the Introduction, a Christian world view can actually contradict a confession of Christ. In other words, we may be claiming to believe one thing but actually living out another.

What is the answer? Hopefully it is becoming apparent: every Christian disciple is in need of a thoroughly biblical world view. The Bible, the Holy Spirit and the natural creation are our reference points and helpers in developing this world view. We will begin to examine some of its contents in the next chapter.

CHAPTER 2

A BIBLICAL WORLD VIEW

The plumb line

To state an obvious, but important, starting point, a biblical world view is one which holds the Bible to be true in all that it affirms.[1] Scripture must be seen as the final arbiter, cutting across all other opinions, preferences and traditions. Once we recognise that each of us is brought up with a world view which is ungodly and sinful to some degree, whether overtly so or in more subtle ways, we need to find a new standard by which to interpret the world in which we live. Repentance is not just about turning from our old paths and from our former ways of understanding, but it defines the new direction. With the aid and power of the Holy Spirit, this new direction is provided by the Bible.

When looking at the subject of the Bible's authority, one need neither delve into unfruitful arguments about infallibility nor make sweeping fundamentalist statements. Instead, we can simply assert that the bedrock of the Christian faith is our belief that the Bible is true and is inspired by God Himself. It is the Word of God which, like a double-edged sword, '... penetrates even to dividing

---

1. This phrase is taken from the statement of faith of the Evangelical Alliance.

soul and spirit, joints and marrow; it judges the thoughts and attitudes of the heart' (Heb. 4:12).

In the language of the prophet Amos (see Amos 7:7, 8), God wants to bring the plumb line of His standard to us, so that we can know His will and understand where we need to change. Using a plumb line can be quite shocking. I remember when I wallpapered my son's bedroom and, following the DIY manual, began by putting a plumb line against the corner of the room. At first I thought I had been sold a sub-standard tool, but then my first-year physics reminded me that gravity tends to be pretty reliable. The fact was that Sam had a crooked room!

Coming to the Bible with an openness to the Lord should be like this for each of us. All our crookedness is revealed and we are presented with a radical clash of world views—ours versus God's. Thus the beginning of discipleship must be an attitude of submission to the Father, a willingness to have His plumb line stand against the way we think, feel and live, and to learn from Him.

Of course, this is neither just an intellectual process nor a case of us striving to 'be like Jesus'. Instead, it involves an internal revolution inspired and empowered by the Holy Spirit Himself, but one with which we must co-operate. 'Do not conform any longer to the pattern of this world, but be transformed by the renewing of your mind' (Rom. 12:2). It has often been noted that the tense of the Greek word translated here as 'renewing' is the present continuous. What this means is that renewal of the mind is not just a one-off experience associated with conversion, like baptism, but is something ongoing. It is perhaps the clearest biblical evidence that the battle of the world views is an ever-present element in life's rich pageant for the Christian disciple.

Whenever we are reading the Bible on a particular subject, we must allow it to refute those world views which are inconsistent with its message. Of course, as biblical Christians we should not be arrogant in suggesting that 'Not only are we completely right, but everyone else is completely wrong'! This is not the kind of humble approach to others which reveals the fruit of the Holy Spirit. Given that all people are made in God's image, it should not be a surprise that even those who have a world view which is opposed to Christianity have something of the truth. This is what I understand Tony Campolo to mean when he says, 'I have seen the enemy, and he is partly right.'[2]

Stripped right down to basics, a biblical world view humbly asks the question, 'What does it mean to make Jesus my God?' What does it mean for the way in which I spend my money, speak to my children, behave at work, or for the way I think and act as a Christian? For this we must look at the Bible.

Creation, the Fall and redemption

Once we have accepted the fact that the Bible is true, and begun the process of letting the Holy Spirit change us, we are ready for the next stage of the world view clash. That is, working out how to apply this truth to the world around us. However, before doing this I want to look a little more closely at the contents of a biblical world view.

There is no way that this book aims to set out all the glorious distinctive features of the vision of life

---

2. Tony Campolo, *Partly Right* (Word Books, 1987).

offered by the Bible. Rather, I want here to examine some of its foundations and suggest a framework to show how valuable a biblical world view really is. This framework, used by a number of Christian writers and thinkers over the past few decades,[3] is that of creation, the Fall and redemption. Its significance lies in the fact that tackling these doctrinal ideas provides the faith commitment which answers the four basic 'world view questions' as I explained in the last chapter. These are the key considerations that steer us through life: who am I?; where am I?; what's the problem?; what's the remedy?

Creation: who we are and where we are
To have a biblical view of creation means that we major on the major issues and not on the 'minors'. In the third chapter of *Whose Earth?*[4] I have argued that some of the hot potato debates surrounding creation over the past century have overshadowed its most important aspects. In some cases, Christians have become so wrapped up in defending Genesis from the scientists and the historians that the fundamental questions which Genesis answers (which are neither scientific nor historical ones) have not been faced.[5]

From the viewpoint of this book, the most important concern is what the biblical doctrine of creation actually teaches. Primarily, it tells us that we

---

3. Most notably Francis Schaeffer and John Stott in the latter's classic, *Issues Facing Christians Today* (IVP, 1984).

4. Crossway Books, 1992. See pp. 35–131 of *Whose Earth?* for a fuller account of creation, the Fall and redemption as set out in the rest of this chapter.

5. This needs to be qualified by making two brief points: (i) that by no means all scientists over the past three centuries, nor all historians over the past century, have been opposed to the Bible and to Christianity, and (ii) that defence of the Bible against those scientists who do not accept the biblical world view is legitimate as science has become a major idol within our culture.

live on God's earth (Ps. 24:1), which was made for Him and by Him (Col. 1:16). It is a world which is essentially good, especially in its whole and completed form (Gen. 1:31), and from which God Himself takes pleasure. (Ponder this thought as you read Job 38—41.) All life comes from the Lord who created the earth from nothing (Gen. 1:2). If the order of creation as set out in Genesis 1 is significant, it is also a world which is capable of sustaining itself without human involvement. God has made the whole universe (κοσμος or 'beautiful arrangement of order') precisely as He wants it, and its form reveals His glory and wonder throughout. (See many of the Psalms, e.g. Psalm 104.)

These beliefs will secure us in a clear understanding of cosmology at a time when many fascinating ideas and theories are being publicised from the world of physics.[6] No scientific evidence has yet been produced to show that God was not the creator, nor is any likely to be produced in the future!

Similarly, the doctrine of creation secures us in a conviction that nature is separate from God Himself, while many world views (like the New Age world view set out in the last chapter) deny this. This is important given the popularity, amongst those influenced by Eastern religions, of pantheism, the belief that everything is God and that this unity is divine.

The creation narratives of Genesis 1 and 2 also tell us who and what humanity is about. Clearly a part of nature—a creature of God and not the creator

---

6. I am thinking particularly of some of Stephen Hawking's ideas as set out in *A Brief History of Time* (Bantam Press, 1988). His theories may actually support the existence of a personal creator God, although as Professor Hawking is an avowed atheist he is reluctant to state this!

Himself—people are described as being made 'in the image of God' (Gen. 1:27). In other words, we are not God, but made like Him; we are dependent upon the Lord for our life, but given authority to rule responsibly over the creation. Our task has been described from the biblical teaching as being 'stewardship'[7] of God's earth. In particular, Genesis 2:15 points to a caring and accountable attitude being required from humanity, as we recognise our calling to interact with the world. Indeed, it is this interaction which makes us cultural, and culture forms an essential part of the formation of world view.

Such a view of humanity refutes the idolatry of humanism—with which we are so familiar in the West—in which people basically worship themselves. It also helps us to see that all people are of infinite value, as uniquely bearing the image of God. This factor should profoundly influence the way that we respond to subjects like abortion, art, child care, education, euthanasia, politics, sexuality, social provision and welfare—in fact almost everything that affects people! It should also mean that we are ready to see the goodness of the Creator in people, whilst recognising the staining effects of sin alongside.

A healthy emphasis on the way people are created will also mean that we recognise each of our own lives to be a whole. Nothing is peripheral in our existence—our work and achievements, our rest and leisure, our families and relationships, our church life and evangelism are each as essential as the other in being human. Likewise the spiritual, emotional, psychological, intellectual and physical parts of our

---

7. It is worth noting that some leading Christian environmental thinkers, like Paul Santmire, prefer to talk of 'care for creation' as more biblical than 'stewardship'. The latter has been used with clear utilitarian overtones in the past.

make-up are all equally important in defining personhood.

In summary then, the importance of creation is far more than just getting dewy-eyed over a lovely sunset (also known as 'the Christian poster syndrome'). Rather it is about a world which has been made whole—a unity enclosing an interconnected web of life. It holds many miracles and shows many wonders in the daily acting out of life's magnificent drama. All of this is from God Himself, the 'Father of lights', from whom 'every good and perfect gift' comes (see James 1:17). Within creation, humanity has been given the special role of making culture and representing the Lord Himself on His earth.

The Fall: our problem
As one looks at the many different religions and philosophies that exist in the world, it appears to be the Judaeo-Christian world view which alone acknowledges the presence of personal and corporate sin. Some faiths appear to have a capricious and double-sided god who seems capable of good and evil. Others put the problems in life down to the slow progress of evolution—assuming that people will eventually rise to a level where mastery of technology and science will cure all ills. Still others see impersonal energies of good and evil wrestling with one another in natural forces, political forces and people's hearts.

But only the Bible fully reveals that the problems of the world basically stem from a choice in the human heart. It is not about a dualistic battle between equal and opposite forces of good and evil, but rather a good world made by a sovereign God who wanted the crowning glory of His creation—

humankind—to choose to love Him. To enable this choice to exist as a reality, the possibility of evil had to be allowed. The rest of the story we know well, as it is told in Genesis 3: from the moment of Adam and Eve's rebellion they died to God and creation was set at war with itself—people against people, man against woman, humanity against the earth itself.

Once people stopped worshipping God they didn't stop worshipping; they simply worshipped something other than God. Idolatry has been a mark of fallen humanity ever since. From crude statues through to materialism and the worship of sex, economic security and political power, the basic choice remains the same for every individual—serve God or serve idols. Never was this made clearer than to the Israelites as they prepared to enter the Promised Land:

> If you fully obey the Lord your God and carefully follow all his commands that I give you today . . . all these blessings will come upon you . . . However, if you do not obey the Lord your God and do not carefully follow all his commands and decrees I am giving you today, all these curses will come upon you . . . (Deut. 28:1, 15).

The significance of the Fall is that it explains fully the status quo—we live in a world which is wonderful and marked everywhere by the fingerprints of a loving God. Yet it is also marred by sin and perverted by the work of God's enemy, Satan. So we see a paradox all around, recognising in people and nature a mixture of goodness and evil. As far as humanity is concerned this mixture is present not only in the lives of individuals, but also in whole societies and cultures.

As the Lausanne Covenant states:

> Because man is God's creature, some of his culture is rich in beauty and goodness. Because he is fallen, all of it is tainted with sin and some of it is demonic.[8]

Part of the biblical vision of life must include an explanation of how Satan's power has such a controlling effect upon individuals and on communities that some of culture is so palpably 'demonic'. The subject of 'principalities and powers' introduced by the apostle Paul in Ephesians 6 is a very lively talking point amongst biblical Christians today. Whichever view we subscribe to personally, we must be willing to recognise that as custodians of God's earth, fallen people have the authority to allow dark spiritual forces to gain a grip over areas of life which we have been called to 'subdue' (Gen. 1:28). These include cultures, ways of thinking and geographical areas, and part of the Church's calling is to 'overcome' these demonic forces through wholistic spiritual warfare (see Matt. 16:18; Luke 10:19; Rev. 2:7, 11, 17, 26; Rev. 21:7).

As in every area of our Christian lives, Jesus is the pioneer of our faith in this spiritual warfare. Consider the powers He faced when He was born into the turmoil of first-century Palestine.[9] There was the military power of the Roman Empire, the religious power of the Pharisees, the economic power of the corrupt Herodian government and the overtly

---

8. The Lausanne Covenant, paragraph 10, 'Evangelism and Culture' (published by the Lausanne Committee for World Evangelisation after the International Congress on World Evangelisation, July 1974).

9. I am indebted to Tom Marshall for this illustration: lecture entitled 'Authority', Cobham, 14 September 1992.

demonic power of Satan. Jesus faced all of these powers: directly confronting Satan in the wilderness, exposing the hypocrisy of the Pharisees, resisting the bullying of Pilate and living in contented poverty. He remained free from the influence of all these powers, saying that Satan had 'no hold' on Him (John 14:30).

Yet at His chosen time, Jesus surrendered to all the powers, as they conspired to frame, try and execute Him. This was the ultimate battle when Satan held Jesus in death for that short time—the darkest hour in eternity. Jesus' victory was won through obedience: sin is rebellion against God, so its antidote must be to stop rebelling and to obey God. In this way death had to give Jesus up and all the powers were 'disarmed' for good (Col. 2:15). It is as we live in obedience to God, enjoying His victory, that we can overcome Satan.

Finally, before moving on to look at the final piece in this jigsaw puzzle of the biblical world view, it is essential that we retain a proper sense of balance between creation and the Fall. Martin Goldsmith has observed that evangelicals tend to major on Genesis 3 at the expense of Genesis 1 and 2, whilst liberals tend to major on Genesis 1 and 2 without giving sufficient weight to Genesis 3. As we look at the world around us we do not fully see what God intended—the Fall was a disaster and its effects are indeed horrible, but we must remember that the fingerprints of the Creator have not been completely erased. If we devalue creation with an overemphasis on the Fall, then we have lost an essential limb of the overall body of understanding.

Redemption: the remedy

The third dimension of the biblical world view which helps us to steer through life is our vision of hope and salvation in the work of the Messiah, Jesus. Quite properly, this is the central focus of evangelical preaching, recognising that the 'Christ-event' of Jesus' incarnation, birth, life, death, resurrection, ascension and His promised return is the ultimate distinctive feature of biblical Christianity.

Yet the fullness of the message of redemption[10] can only be understood fully in the context of creation and the Fall. As I suggested in the last section, if our theology works backwards from Christ then we can end up with a sense of imbalance between creation and the Fall, overemphasising the latter. The result is that the world is not seen as essentially good, but fundamentally rotten, and this in turn serves to fuel theological dualism (the subject of the next chapter). Redemption must be seen as recovering God's intended purpose in creation and bringing fulfilment to it, rather than being a complete 'plan B' without reference to Genesis 1 and 2.

As we think about the 'remedy' part of our world view, many key features could be drawn out. There is nothing in the biblical doctrines of soteriology (i.e. salvation), redemption and atonement which is not relevant to our study. However, I want to focus on just three somewhat broader subjects: hermeneutics, the Kingdom and eschatology.

1. *Hermeneutics*

Hermeneutics, or the science of interpretation, is essential to gaining a true picture of what the Bible is actually saying to us. The concept sounds very complex and profound and at first glance may seem

---

10. 'Redemption' is a theological word which means 'to release at a price', and is drawn from the imagery of a freed slave. In theological terms, Jesus has paid for the liberation of the whole creation from its 'bondage to decay' (Rom. 8:21) and enabled humanity to be freed from being a 'slave to sin' (Rom. 7:14).

something best left to the theologians. But the truth is very different—we all 'do hermeneutics' every time we seek to interpret and understand the Bible. Whether our hermeneutics are good or bad, 'commonsensical' or 'nonsensical', we all have to interpret the Word of God somehow.

A large part of the process of hermeneutics involves trying to get behind what might seem to us to be the 'plain' meaning of a passage of Scripture and then finding out what was the *actual* meaning in the mind of the writer, and what it meant to his or her readers. For example, you may have heard an evangelist quoting the text of Revelation 3:20 when preaching the gospel:

> Here I am! I stand at the door and knock. If anyone hears my voice and opens the door, I will come in and eat with him, and he with me.

This is a powerful passage, but we must realise that Jesus' words here are not an 'appeal' at a gospel meeting aimed at the 'unsaved', but a cry that His church in Laodicea should renounce its lukewarmness.

However, understanding a biblical text is about more than just having the right commentaries. For whilst the formation of a biblical world view must begin with a humble submission to the revelation of God through His Word, we must also know *how* to learn from the Bible. Because we all have a world view, each of us reads the Bible with our 'world view' glasses on. These can distort what we read and part of the 'transformation of our minds' involves taking these glasses off.

Take, for example, the Ten Commandments. Surely these laws, although not the means by which we become righteous to God, show us what He hates in people's lives. Surely each of them speaks equally powerfully to us about how to live in God's world in God's way. Yet with our modern, Western, materialistic world view glasses on, we can so easily read a subtle rank order into the commandments from murder and theft (still very relevant, we think) down to things like idolatry, dishonouring parents, Sabbath-breaking and covetousness (not so relevant in our civilised society, we think).[11] Is this not gross blindness and hypocrisy? Perhaps our world view has made the sin of coveting a forgotten offence against God.

Likewise, when we read Matthew 24:36–41 are we sure that it is the Christian who is to be raptured off and 'taken', whilst the unbeliever is left on earth? Or could it be that the Christian remains on the earth at the 'coming of the Son of Man' whilst the unbeliever is taken to be judged?

Hermeneutics is a technical subject, but one which needs to be demythologised. Christianity is a faith for the people—ordinary people who may benefit fully from the richness of God's Word whether or not they can read or understand theology books. It is the faith of people like John Bunyan who, although illiterate when converted, went on to pen one of the greatest and most widely read titles in English literature, *Pilgrim's Progress*. This book was popular because it was truth made accessible to the common people. We also share the faith of people like John Wesley who, although educated at Oxford University, could communicate Christ clearly to coal miners, textile workers and farm labourers, and disciple them to boot.

---

11. Incidentally, the same could be said of most of the laws, once we do the work of finding out what was really being said.

Put briefly, a world view based on creation, the Fall and redemption needs hermeneutics based upon Jesus Himself, who founded the practice of revealing sublime and timeless truth to the people. For this to be so, we need to give proper value to the Judaistic faith of Jesus—what He called 'the Law and the Prophets', and to the interpretative work of the New Testament from Acts onwards. But the Gospels must be seen as central to our theology, helping us to interpret both the corrective Epistles and the foreshadowing role of Israel in the Old Testament.[12] Jesus must be the focal point of our lives, enabling us to determine our response to our enemies (love them—Luke 6:35), our riches (give them—Matt. 10:8; 19:21), those who wrong us (forgive them—Matt. 18:35; Luke 23:34) and so on.

Such hermeneutics will save us from the intellectualism and rationalism that can spring from an overemphasis on the Epistles, and will keep us in touch with reality. If we do not water down some of the 'hard sayings' of Jesus by overqualifying them with other parts of the Bible, we are more likely to be the radical disciples and the radical Church that most of us secretly want to be.

2. *The Kingdom of God*
So much helpful writing and preaching has been around on this subject in recent years that I will not try to work it over at length here.[13] Suffice it to say that Jesus, redemption and the Kingdom of God go hand in

---

12. I wish to emphasis that neither the Old Testament nor the Epistles are to be relegated in importance. For example, the Law of Moses provides perhaps the most complete application of an integrated world view to all of life.

13. I recommend the chapter on the Kingdom in *Radical Church Planting* by Roger Ellis and Roger Mitchell (Crossway, 1992) as an excellent overview of the subject, and *The Gospel of the Kingdom* by George Eldon Ladd (Eerdmans, 1959), and *Jesus and Judaism* by E. P. Sanders (SCM, 1985) for further study.

hand—when we receive Jesus we find both the liberation of God's salvation and the rule of God's Kingdom coming upon us.

The Kingdom is a wonderful concept embracing much of what the Lord wants to bring to this earth. Explicitly, Paul describes the fruit of the Kingdom as 'righteousness, peace and joy in the Holy Spirit' (Rom. 14:17), but within these terms, justice, compassion, wholeness and reconciliation are all integral. Not only does the Kingdom have wholeness and integrity at its heart, but its scope is all-embracing. Again, as we understand that creation is a whole with nothing peripheral, so the Kingdom is concerned about every area of life, and nothing is truly beyond its scope.

Jesus plainly inferred that the Kingdom could not be precisely located in one area of geography, in one path of life or in one sphere of study:

'The kingdom of God does not come with your careful observation, nor will people say, "Here it is," or "There it is," because the kingdom of God is within you' (Luke 17:20, 21).

Instead, the Kingdom is everywhere that Jesus' disciples bring it to bear. Whatever subject or question we consider, I am sure that there is opportunity to 'seek first his kingdom' (Matt. 6:33) in our approach.

To summarise this in terms of the biblical world view, its aspirations should be seen as very much those of the Kingdom itself. Recognising that the final fulfilment and consummation of the Kingdom of God await Jesus' return, its goal is a truly 'cosmic redemption'—the salvation of God's whole 'beautiful arrangement of order'. Jesus has died to pay for it; we must go and claim it, every inch, for Him.

3. Eschatology

Whilst we seek the Kingdom, we must maintain that the biblical view of life is not one of cyclical existence or of an uncertain future. The end-times picture which the book of Revelation and other prophetic writings paint displays with confidence the ultimate victory of God and His people over sin, pain, death and the devil. Whilst many controversies rage over details of the millennium, the identity of the antichrist and the timing of the παρουσια ('coming') of Jesus, we have more than enough knowledge of the future to shape our present very positively.

For example, if the scope of the Kingdom and of redemption is an all-embracing liberation and fulfilment of creation, surely we can state that God will want to save everything He can. God is unwilling that anyone should perish, wanting 'everyone to come to repentance'(2 Pet. 3:9) and I believe that He wants to save as much of his non-human creation as possible too. The inspiring picture of 'a new heaven and a new earth' (2 Pet. 3:13; Rev. 21:1) should not be imagined in terms of brand-new elements in a different corner of the universe or, worse still, in terms of a spiritualised non-physical location. Rather the Greek word παλιγγενεσια, translated 'renewal' in Matt. 19:28 and Titus 3:5, suggests something renewed rather than something made afresh after the obliteration of the old.

Reading right through the Bible gives a clear impression that this is often God's way. In Genesis chapters 7 to 9 God does not exterminate creation, or humanity for that matter, but saves a remnant. He did not abandon Israel through their unbelief but skipped on a generation before they entered the Promised Land. Most strikingly, He has found a way of saving you and me as poor, miserable sinners. We have been, are being, and will be changed in an inside-out, upside-down revolution of love and forgiveness. If the Lord can do this with us, then surely He can renew the whole of creation.

How then does our view of the future influence the present? An optimistic eschatology—one which affirms God's plans for creation but does not deny the 'birth-pains' to be experienced—should cause the Church to be positive about its interaction with the 'natural' and with the physical world. We should be as active in matters of architecture, art, ecology, human rights and all academic disciplines as we are in spiritual warfare, prayer and evangelism. There is little biblical evidence to state that the former are less likely to be of significance in the age to come than the latter (although we must be very careful not to throw the baby out with the proverbial bath water). Great care must be taken in handling the apocalyptic texts of the New Testament like Matthew 24 and 2 Peter 3 which seem to suggest the destruction of the physical world, but which are actually making a different point.[14]

Eschatology, possibly more than any other branch of theology, desperately needs to be appreciated and understood by ordinary people today. I am not suggesting here that theologians are 'the enemy', deliberately locking the subject into controversies and debates, but the study of the last things needs to become accessible. There can be little doubt that the general lack of familiarity with 'the reason for the hope that [we] have' (1 Pet. 3:15) seriously handicaps the Church in its fight to think straight. A rounded biblical world view must have both its past and its

---

14. See Seaton, op. cit., pp. 89–93 and Tim Cooper, *Green Christianity* (Spire, 1990), pp. 63–69 for more detailed comment on this question.

future secured to enable us to make sense of the present.

Summary

If I had to use just one word to describe the biblical world view it would have to be 'wholistic'. The Christian living in the grace of God and by the power of the Holy Spirit must live a life of integrity. This involves using every gift to the glory of God, being open to Him in body, mind and heart and being whole both in public and in private. Wholistic churches will see themselves as agents of the Kingdom with a calling to make disciples of all nations, bring salt to the communities where they live, equip the saints to bring God's rule to every area of life, and be a light of example by the way relationships are conducted, problems are resolved and needs are met.

It is how this wholistic world view works in action that will be the focus of the remainder of this book.

Exercise 2

A BIBLICAL CASE STUDY

To help in putting some of the ideas set out in the last chapter into practice, let us look at the Bible and see what we can learn. Either alone or with one or two others read Paul's letter to Philemon, particularly verses 8 to 21. I have set out below some brief background comments to the letter which might be helpful before you turn to Philemon. These are followed by a question for consideration and/or discussion. There are some answers on the following pages.

Brief comments on the book of Philemon

Described in one place as a 'wonderful little letter . . . one of the most beautiful pieces of literature in the world',[1] a better outworking of a Christian world view could scarcely be found. Philemon was a well-off Colossian man who owed his Christian conversion to Paul, probably during the latter's stay at Ephesus. He was a generous and hospitable man and had clearly committed himself to Paul's work.

The subject of Paul's letter is a slave of Philemon's

---
1. Rev. G. Currie Martin, *The Century Bible, Vol. 4*, ed. Massey (Caxton, n.d.) p. 29.

known as Onesimus. This slave had stolen some of his master's property and run away, probably to Rome, where he had somehow found Paul. The slave not only found Paul, but also turned to Christ from Paul's preaching. The slave and the prisoner soon struck up a famous friendship, Onesimus becoming a 'beloved brother'; but Paul realised that he must do the right thing and return Onesimus to his owner, Philemon. However, he does so with a heartfelt request on behalf of the slave: first for mercy to be shown to him (offering to meet personally any financial loss owed to Philemon) and second that Onesimus might be returned to continue to serve and assist Paul. Fortunately for us we still have this request.

Now read the letter.

* * *

Question
Consider how Paul's view of slavery and his request to Philemon concerning Onesimus reveal that he is applying the three paradigms of creation, the Fall and redemption.

* * *

Some answers
An analysis of both the situation and Paul's approach to it reveals the following:

Creation
People have been made to relate on the basis of

voluntary association as free agents made in the image of God, and work is designed to be creative, fulfilling and valuable. Note that although Paul knows Philemon is a slave-owner, and that he obviously came to Christ through Paul (v. 19) he does not command the master to release his slave (v. 8). Rather, he appeals to him on the basis of love (v. 9) and Onesimus' usefulness to the Lord's work (vv. 11, 13). His concern is first for the God-given dignity of Onesimus as a man, which has been restored to him in Christ (v. 10), and the renewed relationship he has with his master (v. 16). Only secondly does Paul put in his own, subtly phrased, personal appeal.

The Fall
It is the distortion of sin which causes people to exploit one another and devalues work so that it becomes arduous drudgery. Sin places financial and economic considerations before human dignity and respect for the individual. Slavery, like war, rape and racism, is one of those tragic social evils which Satan has brought to so many cultures over the millennia of human society. Whilst it cannot be proved from this passage, I am sure that Paul sees slavery in this way, but also knows how the gospel works—from the inside outwards.

Redemption
Perhaps the most dynamic and radical lesson in this letter is the fact that Paul is far less concerned with the externals of the situation than with what is going on in the heart. The apostle speaks of an internal revolution which has occurred in the relationship between Philemon and Onesimus. The latter is no longer a slave, 'but better than a slave . . . a dear brother' (v. 16).

Paul sends Onesimus back, not showing any attempt to uproot slavery as such. Instead, he quietly calls upon Philemon to fulfil his responsibility to behave as one who owes an allegiance to the greatest of all masters. Note, in view of all this, that the Bible does not affirm the social status quo of slavery, but rather subverts it by bringing about external change from within.

Most captivating in this episode is the sacrificial attitude of Paul as, to use Luther's words, 'He layeth himself out for poor Onesimus.' Luther continues ' . . . With all his means [he] pleadeth his cause with his master, and so setteth himself as if he were Onesimus, and has himself done wrong to Philemon. Even as Christ did for us with God the Father, thus also doth Paul for Onesimus with Philemon. We are all his Onesimi, to my thinking.'[2] Surely, this reflection of the heart of Jesus is what living biblically is all about.

Other biblical models

Naturally, Philemon is not the only example of wholistic spirituality in action to be found in the pages of the Bible. In many ways, the Old Testament has an even greater wealth of images than the new: the returned captives using team work to rebuild Jerusalem in Nehemiah 3; the craftsmen enhancing the tabernacle in Exodus 30:35ff by skills provided in the power of 'the Spirit of the Lord'; the philosophical questions debated in the book of Job. All of these and more show that if we read the Bible for all it is worth, our spirituality can be enriched and our lives lived more wholly and fully for God.

---
2. Quoted in Currie Martin, op. cit.

CHAPTER 3

TACKLING DUALISM

So far, we have looked at the first step of the 'world view clash' inspired by our conversion to Christ—that is, the submission of our personal way of seeing things to the will of God, as revealed in the teaching of the Bible. In other words, it's about asking the question, 'What does it mean to make Jesus my God?'

The second step is about applying this understanding to the world around us. The challenge that every Christian has always faced is how to be 'in the world, but not of it' (see John 17:14–16). Never has this been a simple matter, but it is only if we are willing to engage ourselves in the two-stage process which I have outlined that we really stand a chance of obeying our Lord's command.

The importance of the process is best explained by showing the dangers of missing out one step or the other. On the one hand, if I get stuck into my politics or philosophy or sport, or whatever, without adequately working out my Christian world view, I might get swamped with another philosophy or vision for life and lose my 'saltiness' (Matt. 5:13). For instance, one could perhaps suggest that some who have experimented with novel theological ideas like panentheism have ignored the influence of the New Age movement, and that those who have preached a 'prosperity gospel' have failed to recognise the idol of selfish consumerism.

On the other hand, if I fail to apply my world view to life by the process of engagement—getting stuck in—I become not a 'doer of the word', but a 'hearer only' (see James 1:22 KJV). I am thus like the man described by James who walks away from the mirror only to forget what he looks like. The truth is only known to be true when it is lived: Christianity was never intended to be merely a set of rational principles and reasonable propositions. It was made to be lived to the full (see John 10:10).

In the final chapter I want to look at some of the hallmarks of a truly biblical world view in action: the distinctive characteristics that it should produce. But before this positive side of the process can take place there is a negative one which should precede it. That is the exposure of what is wrong at present. A wholistic world view needs to expose the ungodliness in the culture which surrounds it before it can truly assert its own good qualities.

If this book was written from an African perspective, we might have to address issues of tribalism or of a 'bwana mentality'; in an Indian context, we might have to confront Hinduism, the caste system or the colonial legacy; in a Latin American situation we might have to challenge syncretism, sexism or animism. I described in the last chapter how Jesus Himself faced the cultural powers that were ranked against Him in first-century Palestine. In whichever culture we find ourselves, there will be a world view which has sway and which is in some way opposed to the gospel. Surely this is what we learn from seeing the presence of the Fall in our view of life—Satan has muddied the waters in every society in some way.

However, as a Westerner, the world view which most subtly invades our culture—and sadly, so much of Christianity—is that of dualism. It is a dualistic lens which must be removed from our eyes before we in Britain can hope to see things wholistically.

Dualism is a complex issue to grapple with and, to complicate things more, there are dualisms that we need to affirm.[1] For example, the dualism between God and His creation is a valid distinction which we need to maintain or we will become pantheists. However, I am using the term here as shorthand for the splits which have been read *into creation itself*.

There are many ways in which dualism could be approached.[2] Perhaps the simplest explanation is to say that its effect is to divide all reality into two different realms. In the language of Edwardian society these are 'upstairs, downstairs' categories with clearly superior and inferior connotations. Human existence is split into an 'upstairs' realm of spirituality, philosophy and other higher expressions of life, and a 'downstairs' realm of work, the physical, material environment and the more mundane aspects of life. Worst of all, it sees the two as essentially in conflict with one another, or as quite unconnected. So we hear some politician deriding Christians who want to influence politics, suggesting instead that they 'stick to

---

1. After all, the definition of dualism is not loaded: 'a dualism exists when there are two substances, or powers, or modes, neither of which is reducible to the other' (*New Dictionary of Theology*, eds. Ferguson and Wright, IVP, 1988, p. 210).

2. For a more thorough-going explanation of dualism, including a look at its historical roots in Western culture (a very important issue to grasp) refer to Walsh and Middleton's *The Transforming Vision* and Wolters' *Creation Regained*, listed in bibliography.

saving souls'. People's lives are divided into the public and the private and there is a strong distinction between the sacred and the secular.

DUALISM—LIFE IN TWO REALMS

UPSTAIRS	—	DOWNSTAIRS
Spirituality	—	Work
Philosophy	—	Agriculture
Art	—	Food and drink
Theology	—	Washing-up

So where have you seen dualism at work? You might have heard people talk about 'being in the flesh' and 'being in the Spirit', as if we can transfer modes of existence at a moment's notice. You might have wondered why some Christians seem rather reluctant to enjoy eating and drinking as if these things were not very spiritual. You might have come across some rather strange and 'Victorian' attitudes to sexuality, which suggest that although God invented it, sex is really a bit dirty. All this and much, much more is dualism: compartmentalised Christianity.

Although dualism is a profoundly spiritual and philosophical concern, it would be a big mistake to believe that it is limited to the life of the Church. Dualism, as I suggest above, is very much an integral part of our Western culture. Indeed, its influence on the Church is related precisely to the fact that Christians have failed to be 'in the world, but not of it'. I am surely not the first to insinuate that the reverse is true: we have been of the world *in* our dualism, but not in it *because of* dualism.

Some historical background

Before explaining it further, it is worth taking a little time to trace the background of how dualism came to influence us so much. (If you simply wish to have the headlines of this history, read the three boxes and move on to 'Dualism and the Church').

History is a bit like a tapestry. Different people, movements and events represent the strands which have been woven together to create the present. An awareness of our history helps us to understand what we see around us and how the whole tapestry fits together. When looking at the history of the Church it can be difficult to comprehend some of the actions and reactions of sincere and Spirit-filled contemporary Christians, and it is sometimes easy to oversimplify why certain things happened as they did. What follows is a bird's-eye view of one strand of this history, with necessary generalisations and simplifications.

We begin our aerial tour of the dualistic influences on our culture in ancient Greece with the seminal philosopher, Plato of Athens.

WHAT PLATO BELIEVED

Plato of Athens (c. 439–347 BC) developed a framework of ideas about cosmology, morality and the nature of life which have been an inspiration to many subsequent generations of thinkers. Today his ideas read like a fascinating mixture of semi-Christian and New Age themes.

However, most importantly for our present subject, Plato believed that every person has a perfect and eternal 'form' which we can tap into by means of our reason. This eternal soul is imprisoned in our bodies, and our sense-experiences provide only a fallible opinion of life around us. Thus, for Plato, a dualism exists between the physical and natural part of us which we experience through our bodies, and a 'higher' existence which we know through our minds, our emotions and our *psyche*. Likewise, on a broader level, there is one realm of life—the material—which we perceive through our eyes, ears, touch and so on and a non-material realm of beauty, wisdom and reason which we discover only through our soul.

In summary, his ideas were no more than some of the first bold and innovative attempts by a fallen intellect to explain the perplexing blend of divinely created God-image and sin-crippled creature which is the make-up of fallen humanity.

You can see what Plato was getting at. How easy it is to sense something pure and noble in an expression of true love, a heart-rending play or the discovery of some fresh truth about life. How uncomplicated it is to blame all our misfortunes and disappointments on venomous tongues, unbridled sexual lust or hunger for status and power. In the last chapter I sought to explain why the tension of creation and the Fall needs to be held together so carefully, lest we throw out the baby with the bath water. Surely this is impossible without the grace of God Himself.

But however we may empathise with the fruitless search which Plato began, the themes of dualism which he sowed were to reap a bitter harvest in the early Church (and in the later Church as well). In the era of the first century—the cradle years of the Christian faith—Middle Platonism was already beginning to taint the gospel itself. The heresies which we know under the generic heading of 'gnosticism' were at their most powerful in the second and third centuries, yet even Paul encountered these errors in Colossae around AD 55.

> Since you died with Christ to the basic principles of this world, why, as though you still belonged to it, do you submit to its rules: 'Do not handle! Do not taste! Do not touch!'? . . . Such regulations indeed have an appearance of wisdom, with their self-imposed worship, their false humility and their harsh treatment of the

body, but they lack any value in restraining sensual indulgence (Col. 2:20, 21, 23).

If the impact of this dualism had been dealt with thoroughly as the pagan heresy that it was in the first century, one wonders if some of the problems faced by the Church from the fourth century onwards could have been avoided. Instead, orthodox Christianity became more and more deeply tainted with Platonic ideas, greatly influencing such esteemed Church Fathers as Origen, Ambrose and Augustine of Hippo. The latter, a brilliant rationalist considered by some to be one of the greatest theologians of all time,[3] became the dominating authority in shaping medieval Christianity in Europe. As we look carefully at Church history and contemplate the effect of the withdrawal from society of the keenest saints into monasticism, with its ascetic tendencies and contemplative lifestyle, the fingerprints of Plato appear to be plain enough.

WHAT IS GNOSTICISM ALL ABOUT?

Asceticism—the rigid denial of normal bodily needs > >
Believers looking for Christ through an inner experience > >
Search for a revelation of God's secret knowledge > >
Christianity became a two-tier affair > >
Two classes of Christians: those who had received the secret knowledge or γνωσις and those who had not.

True, the monastic system encouraged and enabled the transcription of the Bible, and some later

---

3. See, for example, D. F. Wright's opening comments in his article in *New Dictionary of Theology*, p. 58.

monastic orders, like the Franciscans, recovered preaching evangelism and affirmed the natural world. But by and large all of this must be seen against the backdrop of an orthodox Church which replaced its sense of sacrificial, evangelistic mission with a greater and greater desire to come out of the world and be separate from it.

What's more, dualism also made a heavy impact on the relationship between Church and state. In the fourth century Christianity was adopted as the official religion of the Roman Empire after the conversion of Emperor Constantine in AD 312. The Church thus faced a huge challenge as to whether it would continue to be the true community of faith, abiding by the laws of God, or whether it would become the servant of the state, offering moral legitimation to its actions. Sadly, it was the latter course which prevailed and the execution of the first dissenters followed fairly swiftly.

With the seduction and neutering of the mainstream Church into impotence, the baton of truly vibrant faith passed to those in the zealous martyr tradition. Sadly many of these movements, under the subtle influence of Platonic dualism and in reaction to the secularised orthodox Church, became increasingly more other-worldly and ascetic. This polarisation presents a backdrop which, with many notable exceptions,[4] sets the scene right up to the Reformation.

Finally, the theological shadow which Platonic ideas have cast down the centuries are as significant as those relating to Christian practice and lifestyle. A strong emphasis began to be placed upon the *transcendence* of God—i.e. His separation from creation—at the expense of the *immanence* of God—i.e.

---

4. For an introduction to these long-overlooked but important exceptions see Donald Durnbaugh's *The Believers' Church* (Herald Press, 1968).

His presence within creation. Again, to follow a biblical world view requires us to hold both these truths in tension. However, to overemphasise God's transcendence means that the creation is held in lower regard and human work is seen far less vocationally. In other words, if God is 'out there', He has little concern for what I am doing down here, apart from my devotional duties.

Where have you seen all this? You see it in those who stress the kind of 'be ye separate' teaching of keeping ourselves clean from the world. You can see it in ideas about the end times which reduce the importance of the natural world in God's plan. You can see it in a kind of pessimistic 'fortress mentality' of the Church hanging on in a totally corrupt and depraved world, until Jesus comes to rescue us and take us away.

Faith and reason

So Plato has certainly left his mark on Christian thinking. However, significant though the influence of dualism has been in the Church, it has been just as strong on secular culture. It is interesting to note that many of those who are described as the fathers of contemporary thought share a dualistic world view with some of the theologians of the early Church. Outstanding among the former is René Descartes. His work, in the early seventeenth century, brought Neoplatonism into the modern era and, along with the work of others like Bacon and Locke, heralded the 'Age of Reason'. This 'enlightenment' was supposed to have freed European culture from the shackles of the orthodox Church with its medieval superstitions, replacing it with a solid test of rationalism. This test stated that all knowledge can be verified by reason, and that learning occurs through the radical questioning of accepted certainties. This concept saw the birth of the secular culture in which we live.

Naturally, rational faculties are very much a part of our created humanity and must not be shunned. Reason and faith need not, and should not, find themselves in conflict with one another. However, when the route to all understanding and knowledge is defined by what we can rationally perceive, an idol has been created which demands the worship due to God alone. 'The fear of the Lord is the beginning of knowledge' (Prov. 1:7) . . . 'The foolishness of God is wiser than man's wisdom' (1 Cor. 1:25) . . . 'If any of you lacks wisdom, he should ask God' (James 1:5). The biblical world view does not denigrate reason or what might be called 'anointed common sense'[5] but recognises that it must be in submission to the wisdom and authority of God's will. His Word is always the final arbiter of truth and reality—Job teaches that well enough.

So from the seventeenth century to today, the rationalism of what has been described rather pompously as 'Cartesian Neoplatonism' has asserted an ever stronger grip on Western thought. With it has come rampant dualism. The eighteenth-century cynic Voltaire refused to let men talk atheism in front of his maids. 'I want my lawyer, tailor, valets, even my wife, to believe in God. I think that if they do I shall be robbed less and cheated less.'

The dualism of our culture is evident in many ways. At the start of this chapter I alluded to the

---

5. The whole story and character of Nehemiah seems full of this sort of thing.

divide between the public and the private, and the sacred and the secular. Let me now use a populist illustration.

If you are a BBC Radio One listener, you may have heard a programme called 'Steve Wright in the Afternoon'—probably one of the most amusing and original programmes on that network. One of the features of this show is a 'talky bit' or conversation with a 'posse' of Steve Wright's technicians, producers and so on about various topical issues. Being a person of fairly strong convictions about life, I often fantasise that I am part of that posse, debating the points of interest from a biblical world view.

Then I realise that such an idea is fantastic indeed. The reason for this is that the dominant world view of British culture is rationalistic, and the accepted truth appears to be that the existence of God and the veracity of the Bible cannot be proven rationally. When my Christian views clashed with agnostic or New Age ones they would almost certainly be treated with varying degrees of ridicule. Because Westerners are such dualists, any attempt to apply Christian ethics to computer games and women's fashion registers a 'Does Not Compute' on most people's monitors.[6] Perhaps this is why many Christians in the media appear to have so little that is distinct about them: either they risk ridicule for applying their biblical world view or, chameleon-like, they merge into the background of the dominant world view.

---

6. There may be other issues here as well, such as the cynical nature of the British personality and the precise superficiality of popular radio.

62 Your Mind Matters

THE RISE OF DUALISM—AT A GLANCE

4th century BC	-	ideas first taught by Plato of Athens.
1st century AD	-	Middle Platonism influences Christianity as 'gnosticism'.
4th century	-	conversion of Emperor Constantine ties together Church and state, confusing authentic faith and secular power.
5th century	-	Augustine and other Church Fathers subtly swayed by Platonic ideas, setting trend for medieval period.
17th century	-	revival of Platonic dualism during the Enlightenment.

Dualism and the Church

Other illustrations could be used to put more detail on the picture of the dualistic West. However, rather than do this I want to turn back to look at the Church. This, for us, is where the rubber hits the road because (to shift metaphors rapidly!) we must put our own house in order before we can hope to make a difference to the culture around us. After all, whose fault is it that the Church is not taken seriously—ours or theirs?

It always used to puzzle me when I heard statistics from the United States about fifty per cent of the population claiming to be 'born again', and yet on issues like world trade, militarisation of the Third World and economic justice there was not much evidence of the Kingdom of God in American life. (Perhaps our Christian ten per cent of the UK population are not doing too much better!) I remember well the meeting during which I was finally converted to Christ. The preacher was an American called C. J. Mahaney who told of a magazine's reader-survey to find out which were the most influential institutions in American life. He wept as he reported that the Church came in around 13th—well behind General Motors! This tragic statistic was followed by a stunning conclusion: the ultimate in damnation by faint praise . . . 'The church in America is personally engaging, but socially irrelevant.'

The reason for this sorry state of affairs is more than a crisis in church leadership, a lack of vision or weak commitment on the part of church members. Instead, it relates to the gulf which exists between what the idea of Christianity means to the average individual Christian—read the Bible, don't swear, pray, bring up your kids to be polite, etc.—and what the biblical world view teaches us that Christianity is really all about—that is, everything! This is dualism at work in the Church.

I am coming here to the very heart of what I meant in the Introduction by my concern that the Church will not fulfil its dreams or prophecies if dualism is not addressed. At the end of the day every individual has their own set of priorities and interests in life. Before we were Christians these interests generally revolved around a mixture of motives reflecting both our divinely created humanity (like idealistic and altruistic dreams) and our fallen humanity (like meeting selfish desires, whether financial, sexual, ego-centred or whatever). The danger of living in a dualistic environment is that our preaching of Christ can so easily be confined to what dualism would have us believe is the 'spiritual realm', leaving the rest untouched. The dualistic Church will be robbed of its teeth and will struggle to come to terms with interpreting the Bible straight. No wonder some have described dualism as one of the three 'enemies within' the Church, alongside religion and legalism.

Seeing the wood for the trees

Perhaps the clearest way of sorting out the false separations, which dualism has imposed, from the distinctions made by God as He created each thing 'according to their kinds' (Gen. 1:11ff.) has been produced by Al Wolters.[7] He draws a box to show some of creation's major areas, pointing out that church life is different from family life and so on. The lines between each of the areas are God-ordained and they do not divide the creation. Figure A shows this model.

The work of dualism, however, often follows something like the pattern of Figure B. When we see the world divided into two realms horizontally, the danger is that we identify a 'first-class bit' of creation, and a 'second-class bit'.

Rather than two realms, the Bible identifies two regimes—both battling for the same territory, leaving nothing neutral. C. S. Lewis expressed it in this way:

> There is no neutral ground in the universe: every square inch, every split second, is claimed by God and counterclaimed by Satan.[8]

---

[7]. The following tables are gratefully borrowed from Albert M. Wolters, *Creation Regained* (IVP, 1985), pp. 63–66.

[8]. C. S. Lewis, 'Peace Proposals for Brother Every and Mr Bethell', in *Christian Reflections*, ed. Walter Hooper (Fount Paperbacks, 1981), p. 52.

```
┌─────────────────────────────────┐
│           church                │
│ - - - - - - - - - - - - - - - - │
│           family                │
│ - - - - - - - - - - - - - - - - │
│           politics              │
│ - - - - - - - - - - - - - - - - │
│           business              │
│ - - - - - - - - - - - - - - - - │
│            art                  │
│ - - - - - - - - - - - - - - - - │
│          journalism             │
│ - - - - - - - - - - - - - - - - │
│           thought               │
│ - - - - - - - - - - - - - - - - │
│           emotion               │
│ - - - - - - - - - - - - - - - - │
│       plants and animals        │
│ - - - - - - - - - - - - - - - - │
│        inanimate matter         │
└─────────────────────────────────┘
```

Figure A: Creation

```
┌──────────────────┬──────────────────────┐
│ The Kingdom of God│       church         │
│                  │ - - - - - - - - - -  │
│    (sacred)      │       family         │
├──────────────────┼──────────────────────┤
│                  │       politics       │
│                  │ - - - - - - - - - -  │
│                  │       business       │
│                  │ - - - - - - - - - -  │
│   'The world'    │         art          │
│                  │ - - - - - - - - - -  │
│   (secular)      │      journalism      │
│                  │ - - - - - - - - - -  │
│                  │       thought        │
│                  │ - - - - - - - - - -  │
│                  │       emotion        │
│                  │ - - - - - - - - - -  │
│                  │  plants and animals  │
│                  │ - - - - - - - - - -  │
│                  │   inanimate matter   │
└──────────────────┴──────────────────────┘
```

Figure B: Two realms

Indeed this affirms our biblical world view, that God has made everything, sin has touched everything and Christ has redeemed everything. The resulting picture, shown in Figure C, will look very different. It shows that the battle lines are jagged, not straight: different areas experience differing degrees of liberation or bondage (to use Romans 8 language). In contrast to a dualistic world view this model offers an integrated or wholistic world view. Nothing is hived off—salvation will touch everything apart from Satan and God Himself.

	church	
	family	
	politics	
	business	
The Kingdom of God	art	*'The world'*
	journalism	
	thought	
	emotion	
	plants and animals	
	inanimate matter	

Figure C: Two regimes

Six bastions of Christian dualism

To conclude this exposé of dualism let us consider some of the areas where it has had greatest impact. (Once again, I generalise and simplify in order to make the point.) Many godly people have attempted to understand the following issues by careful study of the Bible. However, if I am right about the extent of dualism's impact, a lot of our evangelical theology has been developed in an environment where 'split realms' are expected. Because our world view influences our hermeneutics, dualism leaves its mark.

1. Ethics—personal and community
The first and most fundamental impact of dualism is felt quite simply on the way that we live.

If we maintain the distinction between a Christian bit and a worldly bit of our lives, we have no hope of integrating all the wonderful and complicated elements of human existence into our faith. At worst it can produce what has been called 'spiritual schizophrenia', posing the perpetual question: am I in the flesh or in the Spirit?

For instance, I might find it very difficult to pray when I'm tired or if I'm frustrated with my children. This does not necessarily mean that I'm under demonic attack or in disobedience, but simply reflects the fact that my body, my emotions and my spirit are inseparably combined and part of the unity which is Chris Seaton.

Likewise, I might not quite understand all the detailed implications of buying a jar of Nescafé coffee, or voting Labour, or throwing away my old bottles and cans. Nevertheless, I should not think that these issues, being material and earthly things, are of no spiritual importance. I certainly should not decide to take these actions solely because Nescafé tastes OK, the Labour Party best serves my interests and I can't be bothered to recycle my glass and metal!

These examples might seem extreme or

caricatured, but they might not be. To continue with the example of politics, it is interesting to note that Christian campaigning, right and essential as it is, has thus far been largely limited to obviously spiritual concerns, like the 'life' issue. Crucial social and economic questions like the Poll Tax, the European Community, and housing and transport policy appear to have held less appeal for the Church over the past decade. Perhaps our understanding of 'morality' needs to be redefined.

2. Evangelism

The preaching of the gospel can be seen as making sorties into enemy territory, rather than occupying enemy ground.

Because the Bible shows us that all people are made faithfully to reflect God's image, and to take His rule to 'all nations' (see Matt. 24:14; 28:19), evangelism must stay at the heart of the Church's mission. Dualism can very easily cause us to see evangelism as 'in-grab' rather than 'outreach'. We must reach out to meet people where they are, and to help them to find the Lord within their cultures, not to drag them into our holy club to become like us. Dualism causes people to be in the 'church-business' rather than in the 'Kingdom-business'. Howard Snyder makes this point beautifully in his book *Liberating the Church* (Marshall Pickering, 1983):

> In the church-business people are concerned with church activities, religious behaviour and spiritual things. In the Kingdom-business, people are concerned with Kingdom activities, all human behaviour and everything God has made, visible and invisible. Church-people think about how to

get people into the Church, Kingdom-people think about how to get the Church into the world. Church-people worry that the world might change the Church, Kingdom-people work to see the Church change the world!

What's more, our dualistic view of what is spiritual has caused us to withdraw from so many areas of life that we actually struggle to relate to those outside the Church. It's then a hard job to make them even consider Christianity! We should reflect on this in the light of what God said to Israel about their evangelism in Deuteronomy 4:5–8.

3. Ecology[9]

The lack of a vibrant evangelical witness in the realm of ecology has recently alerted a large number of Christians in the West to the existence and power of theological dualism.

It is perhaps in the sphere of the natural creation that dualism can be seen at its most extreme. If true spirituality is understood as belonging only to the inner life, the natural world comes to be viewed as tainted with the Fall and destined only for destruction. This in turn means that Christians can cheerfully pollute, waste and ravage nature, arguing that such actions are not of direct relevance to salvation.

Before leaving it there, I should add briefly that whilst this Christian attitude has largely failed to challenge the consumerist, technological age in which we live, it is going too far to suggest that this kind of Christianity can be blamed as the main cause of

---

9. See Seaton, op. cit., pp. 98–110.

environmental destruction in our culture.[10] The blame surely lies first and foremost in all humanity's idolatry of progress, greed and their rejection of the Creator Himself.

4. Eschatology
An 'other-worldly' world view encourages those eschatological ideas which see no future hope for the natural creation.

In the last chapter I wrote that a positive eschatology is essential to a biblical world view. The other sort often emphasises a departure from this planet by Christians and, in its most extreme form, can rejoice in environmental degradation. This bizarre response comes from a belief that as the world's problems get worse we must be getting nearer to Christ's second coming![11]

I have always found the idea of what might be called a purely spiritual heaven rather puzzling. Satirised by cartoonists for many years, the image of the age to come being about playing a harp in the clouds seems somehow less than appealing. The Christian version of this suggests heaven as one eternal praise meeting—is this much better?!

5. Employment
Calling and employment are seen as starkly different experiences, if not as total opposites!

Turning to a highly practical issue, dualism identifies that Christian callings fall into two very definite categories: a higher calling to church-based

---

10. For a fuller exploration of this issue see Seaton, op. cit., pp. 47–50 and Chris Park, *Caring for Creation* (Marshall Pickering, 1992), *passim*.

11. The closest to a biblical basis for this is Matthew 24 and parts of Revelation.

ministry or a lower calling to secular work. We naturally recognise that God's hand comes upon some individuals to raise them up in church leadership, evangelism, preaching and the like, making this their primary vocation in life. But for the majority, gifted as they may be in some church-based ministry, their main calling lies beyond the church door.

For the dualist, it is praying for the sick, saving souls and bringing God's Word to situations that marks out true spirituality; baking bread, arranging mortgages and fixing cars just pays the bills. The quicker we can get away from work and into a church meeting/knock on some doors/shout at the devil, the quicker we can get on and do God's work! That infamous phrase 'full-time Christian work' (about which most people are embarrassed, but which we still use) says it all. What it says is that there are those who work full-time for God and those who work part-time for God. Full stop! This is not very helpful.

6. Engagement in music and the arts
Our love for the Creator means that we must love His creation, and affirm all creativity.

For many young people, whose culture is dominated by things like music, fashion and film, the dualistic Christian attitude to art has been a major turn-off. When I was first converted to Christ there was a steaming row amongst evangelicals about whether or not Christians should listen to rock music. Fearmongering about demonic back-tracking and claims that Christian rock was 'popping' the power of the gospel seem laughable to most of us now, although some still share these concerns. Much of the criticism of pop music appears to be based upon personal preference in any case. I can't remember reading much about the demonic influence of listening to Wagner, even though he was heavily influenced by the philosophical inspiration for Hitler, Friedrich Nietzsche, who declared, 'God is dead.'

Dualism is at the root of this attitude, dividing music into the sacred and the secular. I want to know where the creative genius behind the works of William Shakespeare, Wolfgang Amadeus Mozart, Vincent Van Gogh, Charlotte Brontë and Orson Welles came from, even though these people were not well known for their Christian beliefs and lifestyles. Can we not see the Creator in all creation, fallen and redeemed? Surely there is not a Christian F sharp and a secular F sharp—there's only F sharp! When you think about it, there is something a bit bizarre about Christian musicians doing their 'Christian album' and their 'secular albums'.

SIX BASTIONS OF DUALISM

1. Ethics   - spiritual schizophrenia
2. Evangelism   - saving souls
3. Ecology   - a missed opportunity
4. Eschatology   - only visiting this planet
5. Employment   - full-time or part-time for God?
6. Engagement
   in music and the
   arts   - only entertainment

Of course creativity has been warped by the Fall and Christians cannot affirm art which evokes or glories in violence, sexual lust, oppression and so on. But once again, we must exercise discernment, resisting every temptation to throw out the baby . . .

Conclusion

I have laboured the wrongs of dualism heavily in this chapter. Because I have covered a number of subjects thinly, I might be liable for criticism. I recognise that Plato can't be blamed for everything and that dualism is not the root of every problem in the Church (it is, however, a very subtle one). But the enemies within are always the hardest to find and can wreak the greatest damage.

So our biblical world view must first of all expose where our thinking has not been straight and help us to repent—'have a new mind'. What do we do with this new mind when we've got it? This is the subject of our final chapter.

CHAPTER 4

THINKING STRAIGHT FOR JESUS' SAKE

I have said that Christianity is not a matter of mere principles and propositions, but neither is it simply a matter of spiritual highs and gushy feelings. Your mind does matter—therefore, let's think!

There is so much more that needs to be said about using our minds as Christians. In tackling the question of our world view I have addressed just one part of this major subject of the state of the Christian mind. How well equipped are we going to be to face the challenges of a new century and a new millennium? Will we be at the head or at the tail of our cultures? How can we become the bright lights that we want to be, set high on a hill for all to see what the benevolent rule of God is really like?

Clearly, I have not attempted to give all the answers to these questions, but I am sure that—along with loving relationships, fervent prayer, the power of the Holy Spirit, hard work, and deeds of faith—thinking straight and living in a godly way has to be a part of it. Thus, this Pioneer *Perspective* is just a small contribution to help us discover one aspect of our task together. In this last chapter I want to consider the hallmarks that will show we have learned to think straight, and then suggest some steps that we must all take to move on in our thinking.

Hallmarks of a wholistic world view

I am going to assume some of the most essential elements of our biblical world view go without saying. Because space is limited I have to expect that things like a commitment to God, an obedience to His Word, thoroughly biblical personal ethics and morality are taken for granted. This leaves us with aspects of a wholistic world view which are less prominent at present...

1. Opposition to dualism
As we recognise the wonderfully integrated lives that God wants us to live, we will reject dualism and seek to live in spiritual wholeness.

In the currency of our language, the phrase 'spiritual wholeness' thus far seems to have been largely confined to the subject of deliverance and freedom from the power of Satan. Whilst this is an important, if not fundamental, part of wholeness, deliverance from Satan should encourage us to seek freedom in each and every area of our lives. We must pursue an integrity in our humanity and our witness, and avoid all compartmentalisation. With most of us the process of sanctification still has a long way to go and we must constantly be wary of settling on the inside. For example, if we have experienced healing from a past hurt in a relationship, we must never simply sit passively in our new emotional freedom. Grateful to God, we should ask the Lord, in Bob Dylan's words, 'What can I do for You?'

Christianity has been well described as an 'inside-out' faith, for what happens on the inside must always affect our lives on the outside. There is no virtue in existing on a purely spiritual plane (and for most of us it proves impossible). This can so easily result in religion and unreality—the dreaded 'space cadet' syndrome!

Thus, the answer to question 6 of Exercise 1 is that we would probably still be doing what we are doing today if the Fall had not happened. We would be playing with our children, enjoying relationships, farming the land, making things and providing services for one another. Agriculture is agriculture, art is art, computing is computing—but there is a godly way of doing it and there is a sinful and idolatrous way. As redeemed people we should use our skills and our inventiveness fully to God's glory, infiltrating and influencing this fallen society, not simply reinforcing our Christian ghetto.

In summary, there needs to be a root-and-branch review of what we understand to be sacred and what we understand to be secular. Can we validate the natural where it can be redeemed from its sin? Can we enjoy good creativity even though its craftsmen or craftswomen may not share our evangelical creed? Surely it is more about our attitudes than our activities. As Gerald Coates has said, 'Nothing is secular but sin itself.' That seems to me to be a good starting point.

2. Honouring all callings and all socially constructive work

One of the ways we will counter dualism is to find an antidote to the tendency of insisting that a clergy/laity division survives from the old covenant into the new. This is partly achieved by endorsing those who are called to work outside the narrow sphere of Church life.

I have observed two things which concern me in this area. The first is that churches can be slow off the mark to honour those who work in 'the world' (i.e. outside the Church sphere) except when (i) they earn lots of money and start giving it to the Church; (ii) God so anoints and blesses them in their jobs and careers that they rise to a position of influence or status in an organisation; (iii) the work falls into the category of a 'caring profession' like medicine, nursing or psychology or (iv) they are part of a profession with some kudos like lawyers, stockbrokers or senior civil servants. These attitudes smell not only of dualism but also of downright worldliness.

The second concern is that we tend to think that the kind of work people do is not a matter for comment in the Church. Whether we work for arms manufacturers or clockmakers, privately owned schools or state schools, BUPA hospitals or the NHS is a part of who we are and for what we will be accountable when we face God. The utilitarianism that says 'People have to work somewhere' (i.e. so long as it pays the bills it doesn't really matter where) is something which I do not think washes.

Where, in all this, is the sense of dignity for the common worker that comes through in Ephesians 6:5–8 and in Colossians 3:22–25? If we are living wholistic lives, it is surely hard to believe that our work must not be integrated as happily as possible into that whole.

3. Committing ourselves to education

If we really want to hold and pass on a wholistic world view we must be passionately interested in education.

This book is a mere drop in the ocean compared to all the subjects that need to be thought through biblically. Your mind matters because you have unique skills, gifts and callings which nobody can work out for you. To me, this is a part of what Paul meant by working out our salvation while God works in us 'to will and to act according to his good purpose' (see Phil. 2:12, 13). Our whole mind set needs to be dominated by the thought of exploring both how God wants us to understand the work we are doing, and also of how to pass this understanding on to others.

I suggest that there are three areas of education

which a wholistic world view must affirm and influence:

(i) Church training

As we are rediscovering the importance of training people to grow better and more quickly in their gifts and ministries, we must make sure that they are getting a sound world view context as well as practical skills and vision. For example, if leaders, worship leaders, prophets and Bible teachers see the world dualistically, their ministry will reflect this. If they have a truly wholistic and integrated vision of Christ's impact on creation, their ministry will be wonderfully broadened out.

(ii) School teaching

Everybody recognises that school teachers have a huge responsibility for shaping young people's lives. The impact they have on the development of a child's world view is tremendous. How important then that we confirm the value of the teacher's calling and support them in prayer and by equipping them to apply a biblical world view to their work.

Likewise, we must equip our schools workers. Many churches now employ schools workers to function alongside teachers to bring Christian perspectives to the classroom. Whilst proselytisation has long been forbidden in schools, this need not present a problem to the schools worker, because world views can be profoundly influenced without a head-on gospel presentation. For example, in Revelation Church we have schools workers who specialise in teaching about a) sexuality and drug abuse in the context of the HIV virus, and b) development issues and poverty on behalf of a relief and development charity, to name but two.

Each of us who is involved with any kind of school teaching needs to be constantly asking how well our biblical world view is being presented, and how we can teach it in more and more creative ways in the future.

(iii) Studies
Dualism means that Christian students are rarely encouraged to apply their faith very deeply to their studies. I remember this well enough when as a new Christian I was studying for a law degree. I used to feel frustrated at the lack of materials available offering a Christian critique or perspective on the voluminous information I was taking in. Much as I was interested to know what Marx thought about the development of the English legal system, I really wanted to know what God thought about it! Meanwhile, the Christian Union was a nice (and, to me, very valuable) holy club following a narrow evangelistic agenda.

Again, a wholistic world view should validate those who want to study and the Church must see itself as part of the education system. If we do not, we are basically surrendering territory without a fight.[1]

4. Living 'Jesus-style' Christianity
Whichever way you look at it, the Gospels provide a shocking challenge to the way in which we live.

As the Holy Spirit moves with ever greater force through the Church, we have, by His grace, recovered more of Jesus-style relationships, more of Jesus-style evangelism, more of Jesus-style signs and wonders. But, by and large, the issue of our lifestyle still appears to lack much of the edge of Jesus' own example.

Consider His teaching: 'Foxes have holes and birds of the air have nests, but the Son of Man has nowhere to lay his head' (Matt. 8:20) and 'Sell your possessions and

---
1. *The Transforming Vision* has a bibliography which is divided into different academic disciplines.

give to the poor' (Matt. 19:21). Jesus could never be bought, lived throughout His ministry in rank opposition to those in authority and died with nothing more than one item of clothing to His name. He proceeded to say that students are not above their teacher (Matt. 10:24) and went on to prophesy that Peter would also be crucified (John 21:18, 19). Paul's experience as a disciple and apostle of Christ showed the same marks—knowing need, want and hunger (see Phil 4:12), prison, floggings, stoning, shipwreck, coldness, nakedness, work without sleep and danger from rivers and bandits, Jews and Gentiles (see 2 Cor. 11:23–28). And still he rejoiced!

I am not suggesting that either Jesus or any of His followers lived lives of unrelieved misery, suffering and hassle. Surely, His statement about coming that we may have life and have it to the full (see John 10:10), His welcome amongst the 'sinners' (Matt. 11:19) and His performance at the Cana wedding (John 2:1–11) imply that Jesus knew how to enjoy His earthly existence too. But there is something of poverty, warfare and self-giving mission that runs through Jesus' life in a way that, for most readers, is rather uncomfortable. This radical lifestyle is in marked contrast to the superficial religiosity of what many people in Britain experience of Christianity today. Indeed, it is also in contrast to the comfortable conservatism that even those who claim to be radical Christians, author included, often demonstrate.

There can be little doubt that the early Church was part of its surrounding culture, yet it looked radically different to that culture in its economics and lifestyle.[2] What's more, the Church then also knew tremendous favour among the people and grew phenomenally. A 'no

---

2. The exchange of money and goods is a recurrent theme throughout the first eight chapters of Acts.

holds barred' seeking of the Kingdom today, rather than the pursuit of the success and profile of our ministries and our churches, will surely lead us to a more authentic witness to the Lord. A wholistic lifestyle means that we will in no way slacken our emphasis on personal righteousness, overcoming prayer and effective evangelism, but that we will also recognise that public life and private life are inseparable, and that the Kingdom demands every bit of it. Everything we do witnesses to our discipleship of Christ and all our activity seeks the redemption of our cultures. Issues like living more simply, awareness of our consumerism, and models of households must be faced.

We must also see redemption in Jesus' name, or the buying back of what has been stained by sin and claimed by Satan, as the key role of the Church. We must always beware of writing anything or anyone off as 'beyond redemption'—think of the example of Zacchaeus about whom Jesus said, ' . . . the Son of Man came to seek and to save what was lost' (Luke 19:10). God has a habit of writing on those whom the world had written off.

5. An emphasis on life, not death
The flip side of the costly Christian lifestyle demanded by a wholistic biblical world view is that it is based in life and not in death.

The cross of Christ is the focus of history in that it dealt with sin and suffering once and for all, and carved the way back to God for His creation. Likewise, there can be no resurrection without the cross. But having said all this we must maintain that the focus of the New Testament and of Church history is the resurrection of Christ.

Christianity should be enjoyable because the joy of the Lord is our strength (Neh. 8:10). There are many ways in which there is joy in the faith. Firstly, what is more enjoyable than using the gifts which God has given to us and seeing them become effective? After all, our calling is often what we enjoy doing anyway.

Secondly, as I mentioned in the last section, Jesus was unquestionably fun to be with and so should we be. Unless our sense of humour is the result of the Fall(!) it must be imaging something similar in God. Is it too irreverent to imagine the Trinity laughing at some of our mistakes?

Thirdly, life is enjoyable partly because of the richness of our emotional and psychological make-up. Resistance to a rationalistic world view means that we must not be afraid of expressing our emotions. Reading through the Old Testament gives an amazing collage of joy and pain, hope and despair, faith and weakness. Ezra pulled out his beard in anger and frustration, David contemplated suicide in fear of his enemies, the exiles wept when the foundations of the new temple were laid. Shrieks and tears of joy, hilarity at God's amazing blessing on us and sobs of repentance should be part of our wholeness. Accusations of 'emotionalism' are to be resisted as we recognise that the Church in Britain needs much more laughter and many more tears.

6. A good reputation with the people; a threat to the establishment

A second hallmark of a wholistic world view which should spring from our 'Jesus-style lifestyle' relates to the type of society which He founded.

It has been well observed that Jesus left no specific structures in place when He ascended to be with the Father, and few instructions about church life. Indeed, all He left was a group of followers who loved Him and one another, and He told them to await the Holy Spirit and His power. Thus, we must conclude that what Jesus founded was a 'people movement'. He did this, not only circumventing the authorities, but incurring their considerable wrath along the way. Perhaps it was the people power displayed at Jesus' final and triumphal entry into Jerusalem that determined His enemies to kill Him (see Luke 19:28-48, especially vv. 47-48).

As we assess how to respond to Jesus' example we have to decide whether (i) Jesus was a bit extreme; (ii) Jesus misjudged the circumstances He had created; (iii) Jesus was born in a more complicated and tense political situation than that in which we live today; (iv) we are called to be a movement of the people or a part of the establishment. Certainly, it would seem that His first disciples had no doubt that the last question was the most important, and it is axiomatic how they responded.

To be a people movement means that we care about people. Our reputation should be for reaching out to the marginalised, the hurting, the disadvantaged and the lost. We must be consumed to go after Jesus' commission with all our hearts, starting with Jerusalem and Judea, but not forgetting Samaria before we go to the ends of the earth (see Acts 1:8). Where is our Samaria—the home of our traditional enemies? Is it Scotland or Ireland or France for the Englishman, Lancashire for the Yorkshireman and Leeds for the Mancunian? If we want to see God's Spirit move, His people must reach out to their enemies.

7. A robust eschatology
Gone are the days when I used to think that studying the end times was a distraction from the present.

As I stated in Chapter 2, our view of the future must actively shape our present. Both because of its implications for our relationship with creation, and because of its motivating power to help us seek the

Kingdom now, I believe we must hold firmly to a biblical vision of a re-created heaven and earth. The idea of 'going to heaven' is unhelpful and unbiblical. Seeking the Kingdom means bringing heaven to earth: as much as we can, as quickly as possible. Naturally, only the Father knows the day and the hour of the Son's return, but we have a decisive role in making that event happen. 'Come, Lord Jesus' (Rev. 22:20) is not just a prayer, but is also a call to action.

8. A commitment to expand frames of reference

Normally, we can only see things that are within our frames of reference, or the reference points around which we live. It is our frames of reference which help us to understand and assimilate new information. For example, if I am told that the concerns of my Christian faith are confined to those areas directly affecting my walk with God, my spiritual frame of reference is extremely narrow. Growing as a Christian usually means that these frames of reference continually grow anyway, through experience and revelation, but they can be limited by the perceptual environment in which we live. For example, I had read Romans 8:21ff many, many times before I had a clue that it might mean what I secretly hoped it meant—that is, a renewed earth! A wholistic world view will seek to expand these ways of understanding life constantly.

Let me furnish one example fairly fully, to give an idea of what I mean. As evangelicals we must learn not to see the task of so-called 'pre-evangelism' as a cop-out for the real macho thing of bringing people to crisis decisions. Once again, this is not to denigrate in any way the essential work of reaping evangelism in our churches, but is a plea to widen our understanding of the term 'evangelism'. Fifteen years ago you would have been thought a liberal if you held a view of the 'gospel' shared by many evangelical charismatics today. To suggest that the ευαγγελιον is more than just verbal proclamation is still deemed to be dangerous error by some today, but most of us recognise that the good news of the Kingdom must have as many *works* and *wonders* as it does *words*.

Likewise we must now sort out what we mean by evangelism, and how it relates to the rest of life. Take art, for example. The role of art in the creation is not evangelism in the narrow sense of looking to provoke 'decisions': rather it is to bring glory to God by creatively expressing life and reality in a way which introduces people to the Kingdom. Christian drama can be thoroughly Christian without the main character having to get saved!

Surely the Old Testament is another example of a similar thing. If we have rigid frames of reference by which we have to fit every Old Testament story and character into a type of Christ or whatever, we are surely missing the point. Is this book not instead a rich, God-glorifying beginning to salvation history, which the Christ-event fulfilled? Some stories have very close and detailed bearing on salvation or give a rich insight into the Messiah's ministry. Others are perhaps less prophetic, but just as inspiring and beautiful. Think about Esther, Job and Ruth as pictures on the edge of the 'salvation landscape' of the Bible who are wonderful pre-evangelists through their God-centred lives.

9. To honour creativity without worshipping it
The antidote to a dualistic attitude to art, science and social science is to treat it primarily on merit, and not on the faith commitment of its creator. In all these things we must be as shrewd as snakes (Matt. 10:16) as there is no premium on gullibility, but we must also be willing for

some of our sharp edges to go a bit fuzzy. Evangelicals love things to be in black and white, but God has given us a life that is opulent in variety and complexity—apart from the Word of God itself and issues of sin and righteousness, shades of grey are the best we can hope for.

A personal disappointment for me has been with some Christians who have recognised these shades of grey. I believe that their failure has been that they are so willing to let edges get blurred that many right and God-given boundaries have also been eroded. For instance, at certain Christian events, the language seems to become provocatively 'blue', and the content of interviews deliberately cynical, in an attempt to shock mainstream believers. When we no longer clearly distinguish between sin and righteousness, morality and amorality, truth and error, we have been seduced by the world and lie awash in a sea of relativism.

The other excess which we need to avoid with reference to the arts is the sin of idolatry. I heard a recent interview with the director of the National Theatre, Sir Peter Hall, in which he was asked his religion. He simply replied, 'Shakespeare'. Whilst we can admire and honour all creativity, we can only truly discover real values once we worship the Creator, and Him alone.

10. A sense of history

Winston Churchill is famous for saying that history must repeat itself, because no generation ever learns its lessons. A wholistic world view means that we have great hope for the future, but we also know where we've come from.

A right understanding of history, and a balanced view of the scene today, should galvanise our will to prevent the worst excesses of the traditional churches (institutionalism), the evangelical churches (individualism) and the charismatic churches (sensuality). This can best be done by keeping a loose hold of all structures and other 'wine-skins', staying as humble and poor as possible, remaining open in relationship to those outside our own churches and streams and not being afraid to hold paradoxes in tension. Space here does not allow elaboration of these ideas, but they merit more thought.

For those of us who are part of the New Church movement, we must recognise that our history can be traced back through different movements, but that we do not have a long historical tradition ourselves. This makes us somewhat adolescent in our theology and practice. However, we do have what might be called 'a spiritual lineage' in Church history of those who belong to the radical moves of the Holy Spirit on the fringe of orthodox Church history—the Anabaptists, Moravians, Waldenses, and so on. This means we should remember that while we aim to see dualism dismantled, the Church remains the 'ecclesia'—the called-out ones—and that the Church and the state must be kept rigidly distinct. The error of Constantinianism must be dismantled before the Church can be free to act as the agent of the Kingdom.[3]

The other main thing we must learn from history is that revival has not always changed a nation. What I meant in the Introduction about missing some of our goals relates to the fact that we want to see our culture changed profoundly over the next twenty years. For this we seek an outpouring of God's Holy Spirit in the 1990s in the same way that He fell on these islands in the 1760s and in the 1850s and in the 1900s. But we want something that is going to *last*—more than a few days, weeks, or even years, and for this we need to have mind sets that are trained to build church and seek the Kingdom in fantastic ways.

---

3. This paragraph in no way suggests that the New Churches are the only part of the Christ's body offering hope to the nation at this time.

We need an *awakening* of the nation, not just a *revival* of the Church. The eighteenth-century awakening led by Wesley and Whitefield still had direct repercussions in Parliamentary legislation and in missionary zeal seventy years later. That's what I want!

HALLMARKS OF A HOLISTIC WORLD VIEW

1. Opposition to dualism
2. Honouring all callings
3. Commitment to education
   - church training
   - school teaching
   - studies
4. Jesus-style lifestyle
5. An emphasis on life
6. A people movement
7. A robust eschatology
8. Expanding people's thinking
9. Honouring creativity
10. Having a sense of history

How do we begin?

I have always felt profoundly suspicious of any book which suggests a simple 'how to' formula, enabling its readers to be victorious in any given area of the Christian life. But, this personal prejudice notwithstanding, it would be wrong to tackle such an issue as developing a biblical mind set without giving one or two practical suggestions which provide a handle for you to measure your own world view. The way we use our minds will be one of the critical factors to determine what we bequeath to the next generation.

When it comes to handling our own world view clashes, we might do well to consider that faced by the apostle Peter in Acts 10. When God told him to go and tell the Gentiles about Jesus, this was way outside his frame of reference. Peter protested with characteristic stubbornness to the Lord, until he realised that God was breaking him free from his own Jew/Gentile dualism: 'I now realise how true it is that God does not show favouritism but accepts men from every nation...' (Acts 10:34, 35). I believe that Peter's vision of the 'unclean' being handed to him is a picture for us of what God wants to do in the Church—bring down some barriers.

So here are five things we must all do:

A. Think!

Romans 12:2 provides the basic response we must make whenever we find within us something which is incompatible with the Kingdom of God. We must ask God to change our minds into His mind and away from the world's mind.

We must ask for God's help in all our thinking. The mind that you have been given is not there just in case you ever fancy learning a language or doing a crossword puzzle. Thinking is not just for academics, it's for everyone. The Bible is full of thinkers who had nothing to do with formal education, but who had the wisdom of life and of the Holy Spirit. When God challenges our thinking, we should all ask for the Holy Spirit, who 'helps us in our weakness' (Rom. 8:26).

B. Beware of doing the splits

Let's stay open to Holy Spirit to consider whether every area of our lives is being moulded by a biblical world view. We must have no splits between the holy and the worldly: everything belongs to God. This applies to our hobbies, our finances, our consumerism, our relationships and every aspect of our lifestyles. The questions 'What does God think of this?' and 'What are the implications of this?' need to be closely tied in with all our decision-making.

Thinking Straight for Jesus' Sake 91

C. Stay culturally relevant

If we are ever going to make a difference to this generation, we have got to be thoroughly *in* the world. This means we will affirm that which is good in the culture around us. After all, it is well known that William Booth took the drinking songs of London and put Christian words to them. He acknowledged the creativity of the songwriters, asking, 'Why should the devil have all the good tunes?' Likewise, we must expose that which is idolatrous and evil in our cultures. We will not tolerate gratuitous sexism and violence in film, glorification of ego and hedonism in rock music, and self-image massage in fashion.

We must always be seeking to 'enculturate' our message, making it relevant to people where they are at. The way I preach Christ to a teenager in Bognor will be very different to the way I talk to a lapsed Catholic in Belfast. We are best placed to do this if we are actually stuck right into the cultures, not always hived off away from the world. If the missionaries to the Eskimos had not lived among them, how would they have known to translate John 10:11, 'I am the good husky-keeper'?

D. Examine our language and our ideas

By simply asking ourselves questions like 'What do I mean by "evangelism", "the gospel", "the Kingdom", "prayer"?' we allow the Holy Spirit to enlarge our understanding. It can be so easy to get swept along with the euphoria of a church that we don't stop and ask ourselves, 'What do I actually believe?' Of course, this sort of questioning should not be done alone but in fellowship with friends.

For example, a friend of mine was reading the publicity for March for Jesus. He commented, 'What does it *mean* to take the gospel to the nation by the year 2000?' That made me think about it!

E. Ask the question, 'How are we going to make a difference to our nations over the next thirty years?'
This leaves us with the question I raised in the Introduction. Our world view and those of our churches should have some or all of the ten hallmarks I have outlined above. However, even if they do they may still fail to be effective. The reason for this is that, above all, a wholistic world view needs to dream dreams and see visions. It must not be so caught up with the world of today that it forgets we have been called to invade today with tomorrow.

HOW DO WE BEGIN?

A. Think!
B. Beware of doing the splits
C. Stay culturally relevant
D. Examine language and ideas
E. Ask, 'How will we make a difference?'

I believe that in our post-Christian secular culture we have to take a long view. Satan has scarred our society deeply, entrenched his spiritual forces in our communities and claimed our geography for his dark kingdom. A world view which looks to retreat or withdraw from the world will never reclaim it. I want to be part of a Church which will fight tooth and nail to take it back, but live life to the full while we are doing so.

APPENDIX 1

GLOSSARY OF TERMS

The following list includes some words whose definitions you might find helpful:[1]

Atonement
The primary work of Jesus on the Cross. Atonement has restored humanity to its rightful dependent relationship with God. Whilst there have been different ways of explaining this idea, it is based upon the fact that Jesus, as God's *Son*, came to earth and *suffered*, offering Himself as a sacrifice for *sin*.

Constantinianism
The uniting of Church and state, dating back to the adoption of Christianity by the Roman Empire after the conversion of Emperor Constantine in the 4th century.

Consumerism
An economic system, attitude and lifestyle based on the continued increase in consumer goods.

Eschatology
A rather frightening-sounding 'ology' to the uninitiated, this Greek-rooted word simply means the doctrine of the last things.

Hermeneutics
The science, or theory, of interpretation. It involves trying to understand how we can interpret language, indeed all communication, to gain meaning from it.

Humanism
A confidence in the power of human intellectual and cultural achievement. Its emergence as a movement can be traced back to the Renaissance of classical culture in fifteenth- and sixteenth-century Europe, reaching a zenith during the Enlightenment of the seventeenth and

---

1. A fuller glossary of some of the terms used in the book can be found in Seaton, op. cit., pp. 211–227.

eighteenth centuries. Until recent decades, humanistic world views held sway over the hearts and minds of Western society, and it still characterises much of our culture.

Intellectualism
The doctrine that derives all knowledge from pure reason. An overbalanced emphasis on intellect.

Panentheism
The view that the universe is God, although God is more than the universe. It is distinct from pantheism where God and the universe are completely identical.

Pantheism
A spiritual world view based upon the Greek *pan* (all) and *theos* (god). This gives a fair idea of the meaning: 'all is God'. The two basic principles of pantheism are that everything is one and that this unity is divine.

It agrees with Christianity and other theistic (see Theism) ideas in affirming that the world depends upon God. However the drastic difference from theism is that pantheism does not accept that the world's existence is separate from the existence of God Himself.

Rationalism
A system of belief regulated by reason, not authority. It claims to apply the same critical methods to religion as to science and history and subjects all world views to human understanding. This rather arrogant approach to life is a product of the Enlightenment of seventeenth- and eighteenth-century Europe.

Redemption
The concept, first found in the Old Testament (see, for example, Exodus 21:30 and Leviticus 25:25ff), of purchasing something for a price: particularly for a ransom-price. Supremely, Jesus came to give His life as a ransom for many (see Mark 10:45). The idea of 'cosmic redemption' is that Jesus' sacrifice for sin redeems, or buys back, the whole of creation to God.

Theism
Loosely, this denotes a belief in God. It is usually used to distinguish the major religions like Christianity, Islam and Judaism—which all believe in a personal creator-God, who is self-revealing, active in creation and therefore worthy of worship—from other spiritual world views. In particular it contrasts with two other 'isms'. One is pantheism, which does not acknowledge a personal creator-God who is separate from the world. The other is deism, which does not accept that God is still active in the world.

Theology
The study of God or gods, or a conversation about God.

The World
The Greek word κοσμος has a number of different uses in the New Testament, of which two are most important to grasp. The first relates to the broad meaning of the word as 'beautiful arrangement of order'—i.e. it's everything in the universe; all of creation. This is how I understand John to be using it in John 3:16. The second relates to the present condition of human affairs, in alienation and opposition to God, for example 1 John 5:19. Thus, it is not necessarily dualistic to use the phrase 'worldly': it properly means belonging to that world system of which Satan is the prince and which we are warned not to love.

APPENDIX 2

BIBLIOGRAPHY

Chaplin, Jon (ed.), *An Introduction to a Christian Worldview* (Open Christian College, 1986)
Currie Martin, G., *Ephesians, Colossians, Philemon and Philippians* in *The Century Bible, Vol. 4*, ed. Massey (Caxton, n.d.)
Durnbaugh, Donald F., *The Believers' Church* (Herald Press, 1968)
Ferguson, Sinclair B., and Wright, David F. (eds.), *New Dictionary of Theology* (IVP, 1988)
Goudzwaard, Bob, *Idols of Our Time* (IVP, 1984)
Granberg-Michaelson, Wesley (ed.), *Tending the Garden* (Eerdmans, 1987)
Kidner, Derek, *Ezra and Nehemiah* (IVP, 1979)
Lyon, David, *The Steeple's Shadow* (SPCK, 1985)
McCloughry, Roy, *Taking Action* (Frameworks, 1990)
Rocques, Mark, *Curriculum Unmasked* (Monarch, 1989)
Seaton, Chris, *Whose Earth?* (Crossway Books, 1992)
The New Strong's Exhaustive Concordance of the Bible (Nelson Word Ltd., 1993)
Vine, W. E., *A Comprehensive Dictionary of the Original Greek Words with their Precise Meanings for English Readers* (Macdonald, n.d.)
Walsh, Brian J. and Middleton, J. Richard, *The Transforming Vision* (IVP, 1984)
Wolters, Albert M., *Creation Regained* (IVP, 1985)